CW00376999

Compilation and additional new material
Copyright © 2016 by Patrick Logan

The Strange Case of Secretary Clinton and "The Donald"

By Patrick Logan,

Story of the Door

MR. STARR the lawyer was a man of a rugged countenance, that was never lighted by a smile; cold, scanty and embarrassed in discourse; backward in sentiment; lean, long, dusty, dreary, and yet somehow lovable. At friendly meetings, and when the wine was to his taste, something eminently human beaconed from his eye; something indeed which never found its way into his talk, but which spoke not only in these silent symbols of the after-dinner face but more often and loudly in the acts of his life. He was austere with himself; but he had an approved tolerance for others; sometimes wondering, almost with envy, at the high pressure of spirits involved in their misdeeds; and in any extremity inclined to help rather than to reprove.

By way of example, he once had been quite critical of his old friend William Jefferson Clinton about his relationship with Ms. L. However after some incidents involving some randy football players, he had discovered a new outlook. Remarking upon Clinton's "genuine empathy," Starr said, "Leave aside the unpleasantness, his genuine empathy for human beings is absolutely clear."

"It is powerful. It is palpable. And the folks of Arkansas really understood that about him, that he genuinely cared," Starr said. "The 'I feel your pain' is absolutely genuine. Now, that having been said, I think this idea of this redemptive process afterward, we have certainly seen that powerfully".

'I incline to, Cain's heresy,' he used to say. 'I let my brother go to the devil in his quaintly: 'own way.' In this character, it was frequently his fortune to be the last reputable acquaintance and the last good influence in the lives of down-going men. And to such as these, so long as they came about his chambers, he never marked a shade of change in his demeanor.

No doubt the feat was easy to Mr. Starr; for he was undemonstrative at the best, and even his friendship seemed to be founded in good-nature. It is the mark of a modest man to accept his friendly circle ready-made from the hands of opportunity, and that was the lawyer's way. His friends were those of his own blood or those whom he had known the longest; his affections, like ivy, were the growth of time, they implied no aptness in the object. Hence, no doubt, the bond also united him to Reince Priebus, his distant fellow Republican, the well-known man about town. It was a nut to crack for many, what these two could see in each other, or what subject they could find in common. It was reported by those who encountered them in their Sunday walks, that they said nothing, looked singularly dull and would hail with obvious relief the appearance of a friend. For all that, the two men put the greatest store by these excursions, counted them the chief jewel of each week, and not only set aside occasions of pleasure but even resisted the calls of business, that they might enjoy them uninterrupted.

It chanced on one of these rambles that their way led them down a by-street in a busy quarter of Washington, D.C. The street was small and what is called quiet, but it drove a thriving trade on the weekdays. The inhabitants were all doing well, it seemed, and all tremulously hoping to do better still, and laying out their surplus; so that the shop fronts stood along that thoroughfare with an air of invitation, like rows of smiling lobbyists. Even on Sunday, when it veiled its more florid charms and lay comparatively empty of passage, the street shone out in contrast to its dingy neighborhood, like a fire in a forest; and with its freshly painted shutters, well-polished brasses, and general cleanliness and gaiety of note, instantly caught and pleased the eye of the passenger.

Two doors from one corner, on the left hand going east, the line was broken by the entry of a court; and just at that point, a certain sinister block of building thrust forward its gable on the street. It was two stories high; showed no window, nothing but a door on the lower story and a blind forehead of the discolored wall on the upper; and bore in every feature, the marks of prolonged and sordid negligence. The door, which was equipped with neither bell nor knocker, was blistered and stained. Congressmen slouched into the recess and struck matches on the panels; senators took bribes upon the steps; and for close on a generation, no one had appeared to drive away these random visitors or to repair their ravages.

Reince Priebus and the lawyer were on the other side of the by-street; but when they came abreast of the entry, the former lifted up his hand and pointed.

'Did you ever remark that door?' he asked; and when his companion had replied in the affirmative, 'It is connected in my mind,' added he, 'with a very odd story.'
'Indeed?' said Mr. Starr, with a slight change of voice, 'and what was that?'

'Well, it was this way,' returned Reince

Priebus: 'I was coming home from some fundraiser at the end of the world, about three o' clock of a black winter morning and my way lay through a part of town where there was literally nothing to be seen but lobbyists. Street after street and all the folks asleep — street after street, — till at last I got into that state of mind when a man listens and listens and begins to long for the sight of a policeman. All at once, I saw two figures: one a small handed man who was stumping along eastward at a good walk, and the other, Megyn Kelly of Fox news who was running as hard as she was able down a cross street. Well, sir, the two ran into one another naturally enough at the corner; and then came the horrible part of the thing; for the man trampled calmly over Megyn's body and left her screaming on the ground. It sounds nothing to hear, but it was hellish to see.

It wasn't like a man; it was some damned reality TV star. I gave a view, took to my heels, collared the gentleman, and brought him back to where there was already quite a group about the screaming news person. He was perfectly cool and made no resistance, but gave me one orange faced look, so ugly that it brought out the sweat on me like running. The people who had turned out were the Democrats; and pretty soon, the doctor, for whom she had been sent, put in his appearance. Well, she was not much the worse, more frightened, according to the Sawbones; and there you might have supposed would be an end to it. But there was one curious circumstance. I had taken a loathing to my gentleman at first sight. So had the Democrats, which was only natural. But the doctor's case was what struck me. He was the usual cut-and-dry apothecary, of no particular age and color, with a strong New York accent, and about as emotional as a bagpipe. Well, sir, he was like the rest of us; every time he looked at my prisoner, I saw that Sawbones turn sick and white with the desire to kill him. I knew what was in his mind, just as he knew what was in mine; and killing being out of the question, we did the next best. We told the man we could and would make such a scandal out of this, as should make his poll numbers sink from one end of the country to the other. If he had any friends or any credit, we undertook that he should lose them. And all the time, as we were pitching it in red hot, we were keeping the women off him as best we could, for they were as wild as harpies with blood coming from, well whatever. I never saw a circle of such hateful faces; and there was the man in the middle, with a kind of black, sneering coolness — frightened too, I could see that — but carrying it off, sir, really like Satan. 'If you choose to make capital out of this accident,' said he, 'I am naturally a great businessman – the greatest businessman. Everyone says so, but I wish to avoid a scene,' says he. 'Name your figure and my charitable foundation will pay it – just ask my son Eric.' Well, he would have clearly liked to stick out; but there was something about the lot of us that meant mischief, and at last he struck. The next thing was to get the money; and where do you think he took us but to the Trump Jet and then New York City. There he carried us but to that place with the ten foot high golden letters on the Building? — whipped the undocumented doorman, went in, and presently came back with the matter of ten pounds in Trump steaks and a check for the balance, drawn payable to bearer and signed with a name that I can't mention, though it's one of the points of my story, but it was a name at least very well-known and often printed. The figure was stiff, but the signature was good for more than that if it was only genuine. I took the liberty of pointing out to my gentleman that the whole business looked apocryphal, and that a man does not, in real life, walk into building at four in the morning and come out of it with a woman's check for this large a sum. But he was quite easy and sneering. 'Set your small, loser mind at rest,' says he, 'I will stay with you till the banks open and cash the check myself because I am so rich, like billions of dollars rich. Richer than everybody in the world. I'm Huge. Everybody knows it.' So we all set off, and next day, when we had breakfasted, went in a body to the bank. I gave in the check myself and said I had every reason to believe it was a forgery. Not a bit of it. The check was genuine.'

'Tut-tut,' said Mr. Starr.

'I see you feel as I do,' said Reince Priebus. 'Yes, it's a bad story. For my man was a fellow that nobody could have to do with, a really damnable man; and the person that drew the check is the very pink of the proprieties, celebrated too, and (what makes it worse) one of your Democrats who does what they call good. Blackmail, I suppose; an honest woman paying through the nose for some of the capers of her youth, or those of her husband as you are well aware. Though even that, you know, is far from explaining all,' he added, and with the words fell into a vein of musing.

From this, he was recalled by Mr. Starr asking rather suddenly:' and you don't know if the drawer of the check lives there?'

'A likely place, isn't it?' returned Reince Priebus. 'But I happen to have noticed her address; she lives in some square or other.'

'And you never asked about the — place with the door?' said Mr. Starr.

'No, sir: I had a delicacy,' was the reply. 'I feel very strongly about putting questions; it partakes too much of the style of the Day of Judgment. You start a question, and it's like starting a stone. No, sir, I make it a rule of mine: the more it looks like it polls poorly, the less I ask.'

'A very good rule, too,' said the lawyer.

'But I have studied the place for myself,' continued Reince Priebus.' It seems scarcely a house. There is no other door, and nobody goes in or out of that one but, once in a great while, the gentleman of my adventure. There are three windows looking on the court on the first floor; none below; the windows are always shut but they're clean. And then there is a chimney which is generally smoking; so somebody must live there. And yet it's not so sure; for the buildings are so packed together about that court, that it's hard to say where one ends and another begins.'

The pair walked on again for a while in silence; and then, 'Priebus,' said Mr. Starr, 'that's a good rule of yours.'

'Yes, I think it is,' returned Priebus.

'But for all that,' continued the lawyer, 'there's one point I want to ask: I want to ask the name of that man who walked over the newswoman.'

'Well,' said Reince Priebus, 'I can't see what harm it would do. It was a man of the name of Donald J. Trump.'

'H'm,' said Mr. Starr. 'What sort of a man is he to see?'

'He is not easy to describe. There is something wrong with his appearance; something displeasing, something downright detestable. I never saw a man I so disliked, and yet I scarce know why I felt he might run for President as a Republican. He must be deformed somewhere; he gives a strong feeling of deformity, although I couldn't specify the point. He's an extraordinary-looking man, and yet I really can name nothing that does not offend me about his ghastly appearance. No, sir; I can make no hand of it; I can't describe him. And it's not for want of memory; for I declare I can see him this moment.'

Mr. Starr again walked some way in silence and obviously under a weight of consideration.
'You are sure he used a key?' he inquired at last.
'My dear sir...' began Priebus, surprised out of himself.

'Yes, I know,' said Starr; 'I know it must seem strange. The fact is, if I do not ask you the name of the other party, it is because I know it already. You see, Reince, your tale has gone home. If you have been inexact in any point, you had better correct it.'

'I think you might have warned me,' returned the other, with a touch of sullenness. 'But I have been pedantically ex- act, as you call it. The fellow had a key; and what's more, he has it still. I saw him use it, not a week ago.

Mr. Starr sighed deeply but said never a word, and the young man presently resumed. 'Here is another lesson to say nothing,' said he. 'I am ashamed of my long tongue. Let us make a bargain never to refer to this again.'

'With all my heart,' said the lawyer. 'I shake hands on that, Reince.'

SEARCH FOR "The Donald"

THAT evening Mr. Starr came home to his house in somber spirits and sat down to dinner without relish. It was his custom of a Sunday, when this meal was over, to sit close by the fire, a volume of some dry divinity on his reading desk until the clock of the neighboring church rang out the hour of twelve when he would go soberly and gratefully to bed. On this night, however, as soon as the cloth was taken away, he took up a candle and went into his room. There he opened his safe, took from the most private part of it a document endorsed on the envelope as former Secretary of State Hillary Clinton's Will, and sat down with a clouded brow to study its contents.

The will was madness, for Mr. Starr, though he took charge of it now that it was made, had refused to lend the least assistance in the making of it; it provided not only that, in case of the decease of Hillary Clinton, all her possessions were to pass into the hands of her 'friend and benefactor Donald Trump,' but that in case of Secretary Clinton's 'disappearance or unexplained absence for any period exceeding three calendar months,' it said Donald Trump should step into the said Hillary Clinton's shoes without further delay and free from any burthen or obligation, beyond the payment of a few small sums to the members of h e r household, which he would then cut by 50% for what he claimed was poor service. This document had long been the lawyer's eyesore. It offended him both as a lawyer and as someone who paid his debts promptly. And hitherto it was his ignorance of "The Donald" that had swelled his indignation; now, by a sudden turn, it was his knowledge. It was already bad enough when the name was but a name of which he could watch on an episode of "the Apprentice". It was worse when it began to be clothed upon with detestable attributes; and out of the shifting, insubstantial mists that had so long baffled his eye, there leaped up the sudden, definite presentment of a fiend.

'I thought it was madness,' he said, as he replaced the obnoxious paper in the safe, 'and now I begin to fear it is disgrace.'

With that he blew out his candle, put on a great-coat, and set forth again to Washington, D.C., that citadel of lies, where his friend, the great President Obama, lived in the White House. 'If anyone knows, it will be Obama,' he had thought. The solemn secret service agent knew and welcomed him; he was subjected to no stage of delay but ushered direct from the door to the dining room where President Obama sat alone over his wine. This was a hearty, healthy, dapper, gentleman, with a shock of hair prematurely turning white, and a cool and decided manner.

At sight of Mr. Starr, he sprang up from his chair in fear he was going to launch another investigation but then welcomed him with both hands. The geniality, as was the way of the man, was somewhat stiff to the eye; as it reposed on no feeling. For these two were not old friends, not old mates, but both thorough respecters of themselves, and, what does not always follow, men who thoroughly hated each other's company.

After a little rambling talk, the lawyer led up to the subject which so disagreeably preoccupied his mind.

'I suppose, Obama,' Starr said, 'you and I must be the two oldest friends that Hillary Clinton has?' 'Definitely not you,' chuckled President Obama. 'But I suppose we are now. And what of that? I see little of her now that she is on the campaign trail.'

Indeed?' said Starr. 'I thought you had a bond of common interest.'

'We had,' was the reply. 'But it is months since Hillary Clinton became too "conservative" for me. She began to go wrong, wrong in mind; and though of course, I continue to take an interest in her for old sake's, as they say, I see and I have seen devilish little of the woman. Such un-progressive balderdash,' added the President, flushing suddenly purple, 'would have estranged FDR.'

This little spirit of temper was somewhat of a relief to Mr. Starr. 'They have only differed on some point of progressive,' he thought; and being a man of no liberal passions (except in the matter of conveyancing), he even added: 'It is nothing worse than that!' He gave his friend a few seconds to recover his composure, and then approached the question he had come to put. 'Did you ever come across a protégé of hers — one Trump?' he asked.

'Trump?' repeated Obama. 'The Bankrupt casino reality TV guy. No. Never heard of him.'
That was the amount of information that the lawyer carried back with him to the great, dark bed on which he tossed to and fro, until the small hours of the morning began to grow large. It was a night of little ease to his toiling mind, toiling in mere darkness and besieged by questions.

Six o 'clock struck on the bells of the church that was so conveniently near to Mr. Starr's dwelling, and still he was digging at the problem. Hitherto it had touched him on the intellectual side alone; but now his imagination also was engaged, or rather enslaved; and as he lay and tossed in the gross darkness of the night and the curtained room, Reince Priebus's tale went by before his mind in a scroll of lighted pictures.

He would be aware of the great field of lobbyists of a nocturnal city; then of the figure of a man walking swiftly; then of a Megyn Kelly running; and then that orange Juggernaut trod the woman down and passed on regardless of her screams. Or else he would see a room in a rich house, where his friend lay asleep, dreaming and smiling at her dreams; and then the door of that room would be opened, the curtains of the bed plucked apart, the sleeper recalled, and lo, there would stand by his side a figure to whom power was given, and even at that dead hour, she must rise and do its bidding. The figure in these two phases haunted the lawyer all night; and if at any time he dozed over, it was but to see it glide more stealthily through sleeping houses, or move the more swiftly and still the more swiftly, even to dizziness, through wider labyrinths of city, and at every street-corner crush someone from the "Dishonest Media" and leave them screaming.

And still the figure had an orange face by which he might know it; even in his dreams, it had an orange face, one that baffled him and melted before his eyes; and thus it was that there sprang up and grew apace in the lawyer's mind a singularly strong, almost an inordinate, curiosity to behold the horrific features of "The Donald". If he could but once set eyes on him, he thought the mystery would lighten and perhaps roll altogether away, as was the habit of mysterious things when well examined. He might see a reason for his friend's strange preference or bondage (call it which you please for Trump definitely enjoyed bondage) and even for the startling clause of the will. At least it would be a face worth seeing: the face of a man who was without bowels of mercy: a face which had but to show itself to raise up, in the mind of the impressionable Priebus, a spirit of enduring hatred, yet an odd desire for Reince to support his run for President.

From that time forward, Mr. Starr began to haunt the door in the by-street of shops. In the morning before office hours, at noon when business was plenty, and time scarce, at night under the face of the fogged city moon, by all lights and at all hours of solitude or concourse, the lawyer was to be found on his chosen post.

'If he is "The Donald",' he had thought, 'I shall be the Independent Investigator.' And at last his patience was rewarded. It was a fine dry night; frost in the air; the streets as clean as a ballroom floor; the lamps, unshaken, by any wind, drawing a regular pattern of light and shadow. By ten o'clock, when the shops were closed, the by-street was very solitary and, in spite of the low growl from all round, very silent. Small sounds carried far; domestic sounds out of the houses were clearly audible on either side of the roadway, and the rumor of the approach of any passenger preceded him by a long time. Mr.

Starr had been some minutes at his post when he was aware of an odd, light footstep drawing near. In the course of his nightly patrols, he had long grown accustomed to the quaint effect with which the footfalls of a single person, while he is still a great way off, suddenly spring out distinct from the vast hum and clatter of the city. Yet his attention had never before been so sharply and decisively arrested; and it was with a strong, superstitious provision of success that he withdrew into the entry of the court.

The steps drew swiftly nearer and swelled out suddenly louder as they turned the end of the street. The lawyer, looking forth from the entry, could soon see what manner of man he had to deal with. He was overweight and had extremely small hands, wearing a red "Make America Great Again" baseball cap, and the look of him, even at that distance, went somehow strongly against the watcher's inclination. But he made straight for the door, crossing the roadway to save time; and as he came, he drew a key from his pocket like one approaching home.

Mr. Starr stepped out and touched him on the shoulder as he passed.' "The Donald", I think?'

"The Donald" shrank back with a hissing intake of the breath. But his fear was only momentary; and though he did not look the lawyer in the face, he answered coolly enough:

'That is my name. Don't wear it our loser. What do you want?'

'I see you are going in,' returned the lawyer. 'I am an old friend of Secretary Clinton's and her husband — Mr. Starr- you must have heard my name, and meeting you so conveniently, I thought you might admit me.'

'You will not find Secretary Clinton or her husband; she is from home,' replied "The Donald", blowing in the key. And then suddenly, but still without looking up, 'How did you know me?' he asked.

'On your side,' said Mr. Starr, 'will you do me a favor?'

'What's in it for me,' replied the other. 'What shall it be?'

'Will you let me see your face?' asked the lawyer.

"The Donald" appeared to hesitate, and then, as if upon some sudden reflection, fronted about with an air of defiance; and the pair stared at each other pretty fixedly for a few seconds. He exclaimed, "I am so good looking and you are really lucky to get to look at the best face ever".

'Now I shall know you again,' said Mr. Starr.' It may be useful.'

'Yes,' returned "The Donald", 'it is as well we have, met; and now that you know how incredibly handsome I am, the most handsome face you ever saw in fact, you also should have my address.' And he gave the address of Trump Tower.

'Good God!' thought Mr. Starr,' can he, too, have been thinking of the will?' But he kept his feelings to himself and only grunted in acknowledgment of the address.

'And now,' said the other, 'how did you know me?'

'From TV,' was the reply.

'Oh, the Apprentice – the number one show on television?'

'Yes, and we have common friends, said Mr. Starr.

'Common friends?' echoed "The Donald", a little hoarsely.' Who are they?'

'Clinton, for instance,' said the lawyer.

'She never told you,' cried "The Donald", with a flush of anger.' I did not think you would have lied.'

'Come,' said Mr. Starr, 'that is not fitting language.' The other snarled aloud into a savage laugh; and the next moment, with extraordinary quickness, he had unlocked the door and disappeared into the house.

The lawyer stood a while when "The Donald" had left him, the picture of disquietude. Then he began slowly to mount the street, pausing every step or two and putting his hand to his brow like a man in mental perplexity. The problem he was thus debating as he walked, was one of a class that is rarely solved. "The Donald" was orange and o b e s e, he gave an impression of deformity without any nameable malformation, he had a displeasing smile, he had borne himself to the lawyer with a sort of murderous mixture of timidity and boldness, and he spoke with a husky, loud and somewhat incoherent voice; all these were points against him, but not all of these together could explain the hitherto unknown disgust, loathing, and fear with which Mr. Starr regarded him. 'There must be something else,' said the perplexed gentleman. 'There is something more if I could find a name for it. God bless me, the man seems hardly human! Something troglodytic, shall we say? Or can it be the old story of Secretary Fell? Is it the mere radiance of a foul soul that thus transpires through, and transfigures, its clay continent? The last, I think; for, O my poor Hillary Clinton, if ever I read Satan's signature upon a face, it is on that of your new friend.'

Round the corner from the by-street, there was a square of ancient, handsome houses, now for the most part decayed from their high estate and let in flats and chambers to all sorts and conditions of men: map-engravers, architects, shady lawyers, and the agents of obscure enterprises. One house, however, second from the corner, was still occupied entire; and at the door of this, which wore a great air of wealth and comfort, though it was now plunged in darkness except for the fan-light, Mr. Starr stopped and knocked. Bill Clinton opened the door.

Is Mrs. Clinton at home, Bill?' asked the lawyer.

'I will see, Mr. Starr,' said Bill, admitting the visitor, as he spoke, into a large, low-roofed, comfortable hall, paved with flags, warmed (after the fashion of a country house) by a bright, open fire, and furnished with costly cabinets of oak. 'Will you wait here by the fire, sir? or shall I give you a light in the dining room?'

'Here, thank you,' said the lawyer, and he drew near and leaned on the tall fender. This hall, in which he was now left alone, was a pet fancy of his friend the doctor's; and Starr himself was wont to speak of it as the pleasantest room he knew. But to-night there was a shudder in his blood; the face of Trump sat heavy on his memory; he felt (what was rare with him) nausea and distaste of life; and in the gloom of his spirits, he seemed to read a menace in the flickering of the firelight on the polished cabinets and the uneasy starting of the shadow on the roof. He was ashamed of his relief when Bill presently returned to announce that Secretary Clinton was gone out.

'I saw "The Donald" go in by the old secret donor greeting room door, Bill,' he said. 'Is that right, when Secretary Clinton is from home?'

'Quite right, Mr. Starr, sir,' replied Bill. '"The Donald" has a key.'

'Your wife seems to repose a great deal of trust

in that young man, Bill,' resumed the other musingly.

'Yes, sir, she does indeed,' said Bill. 'We have all orders to obey him.'

'I do not think I ever met "The Donald"?' asked Starr.

O, dear no, sir. He never dines here,' replied the butler.
'Indeed we see very little of him on this side of the house; he mostly comes and goes in secret.'
'Well, good-night, Bill.'

'Good-night, Mr. Starr.' And the lawyer set out homeward with a very heavy heart.' Poor Clinton,' he thought, 'my mind misgives me she is in deep waters! Her husband was wild when he was young; a long while ago to be sure; but in the law of God, there is no statute of limitations. Ay, it must be that; the ghost of some old sin, the cancer of some concealed disgrace: punishment coming, years after memory has forgotten and self-love condoned the fault.'

And the lawyer, scared by the thought, brooded a while on his own past, groping in all the corners of memory, lest by chance some Jack-in-the-Box of an old iniquity about football players should leap to light there. He told everyone his past was fairly blameless; few men could sell the rolls of their life with less apprehension; yet he was humbled to the dust by the many ill things he had done, and raised up again into a sober and fearful gratitude by the many that he had come so near to doing, yet avoided. And then by a return to his former subject, he conceived a spark of hope. 'This Master Trump, if he were studied,' thought he, 'must have secrets of his own; black secrets, by the look of him; secrets compared to which poor Clinton's worst would be like sunshine. Things cannot continue as they are. It turns me cold to think of this creature stealing like a thief to Harry's bedside; poor Harry, what a wakening! And the danger of it; for if this Trump suspects the existence of the will, he may grow impatient to inherit. Ay, I must put my shoulder to the wheel if Clinton will but let me,' he added, 'if Clinton will only let me.' For once more he saw before his mind's eye, as clear as a transparency, the strange clauses of the will.

Secretary Clinton was quite at ease

A FORTNIGHT later, by excellent good fortune, the doctor gave one of his pleasant dinners to some five or six old cronies, all intelligent, reputable men and all judges of good wine; and Mr. Starr so contrived that he remained behind after the others had departed. This was no new arrangement, but a thing that had befallen many scores of times. Where Starr was liked, he was liked by Republicans. Hosts loved to detain the dry lawyer when the light-hearted and the loose-tongued had already their foot on the threshold; they liked to sit a while in his unobtrusive company, practicing for solitude, sobering their minds in the man's rich complaints about liberals after the expense and strain of gaiety. To this rule, Secretary Clinton was an exception; and as she now sat on the opposite side of the fire — a pantsuited, well-made, woman of sixty-eight, with something of a mechanical cast perhaps, but every mark of capacity and kindness — you could see by her looks that she hated Mr. Starr, but presented a fake and warm affection.

'I have been wanting to speak to you, Secretary Clinton,' began the latter. 'You know that will of yours?'

A close observer might have gathered that the topic was distasteful, but the Secretary carried it off gaily. 'My poor Starr,' said he, 'you are unfortunate in such a client. I never saw a man as distressed as you were by my will; unless it were that hide-bound pedant, Obama, at what he called my neo-liberal heresies. Oh, I know he's a good fellow — you needn't frown — an excellent fellow, and I always mean to see more of him; but a hide-bound pedant for all that; an ignorant, blatant pedant. I was never more disappointed in any man than Obama.'

'You know I never approved of it,' pursued Starr, ruthlessly disregarding the fresh topic.

'My will? Yes, certainly, I know that,' said the Secretary, a trifle sharply. 'You have told me so.'

'Well, I tell you so again,' continued the lawyer. 'I have been learning something of Trump.'

The robot-like face of Secretary Clinton grew pale to the very lips, and there came a blackness about her eyes. 'I do not care to hear more,' said she. 'This is a matter I thought we had agreed to drop.'

'What I heard was abominable,' said Starr.
'It can make no change. You do not understand my position,' returned the Secretary, with a certain incoherency of manner. 'I am painfully situated, Starr; my position is a very strange — a very strange one. It is one of those affairs that cannot be mended by talking.'

'Clinton,' said Starr, 'you know me: I am a man to be trusted. Ask your husband. Make a clean breast of this in confidence, and I make no doubt I can get you out of it.'

'My good Starr,' said the Secretary, 'this is very good of you, this is downright good of you, and I cannot find words to thank you in. I don't believe you fully; I would trust you as far as I can through you, ay, if I could make the choice; but indeed it isn't what you fancy; it is not so bad as that; and just to put your good heart at rest, I will tell you one thing: the moment I choose, I can be rid of "The Donald". I give you my hand upon that, and I thank you again and again; and I will just add one little word, Starr, that I'm sure you'll take in good part: this is a private matter, and I beg of you to let it sleep.'

Starr reflected a little, looking into the fire.

'I have no doubt you are perfectly right,' he said, at last, getting to his feet.

'Well, but since we have touched upon this business, and for the last time I hope,' continued the Secretary, 'there is one point I should like you to understand. I have really a very great interest in poor Trump. I know you have seen him; he told me so, and I fear he was rude. But, I do sincerely take a great, a very great interest in that annoying man; and if I am taken away, Starr, I wish you to promise me that you will bear with him and get his rights for him. I think you would if you knew all, and it would be a weight off my mind if you would promise.'

'I can't pretend that I shall ever like him,' said the lawyer.

'Who could? I don't ask that,' pleaded Clinton, laying her hand upon the other's arm; 'I only ask for justice; I only ask you to help him for my sake, when I am no longer here.'

Starr heaved an irrepressible sigh. 'Well,' said he, 'I Promise.

THE RYAN MURDER CASE

NEARLY a year later, in the month of October 2016, Washington was startled by a crime of singular ferocity and rendered all the more notable by the high position of the victim. The details were few and startling. A maid servant living alone in a house not far from the Capitol had gone up-stairs to bed about eleven. Although a fog rolled over the city in the small hours, the early part of the night was cloudless, and the lane, which the maid's window overlooked, was brilliantly lit by the full moon. It seems she was romantically given, for she sat down upon her box, which stood immediately under the window, and fell into a dream of musing. Never (she used to say, with streaming tears, when she narrated that experience), never had she felt more at peace with all men or thought more kindly of the world. And as she so sat she became aware of a congressman with dark hair, drawing near along the lane, and advancing to meet him, another and very small gentleman, to whom at first she paid less attention. When they had come within speech (which was just under the maid's eyes) the handsome man bowed and accosted the other with a very pretty manner of politeness. It did not seem as if the subject of his address were of great importance; indeed, from his pointing, it sometimes appeared as if he were only inquiring his way; but the moon shone on his face as he spoke, and the girl was pleased to watch it, it seemed to breathe such an innocent and old-world kindness of disposition, yet with something high too, as of a well-founded self-content. Presently her eye wandered to the other, and she was surprised to recognize him as "The Donald", who had once visited her master and for whom she had conceived a dislike and who always hit on her. He had in his hand a bottle of Trump Vodka, with which he was trifling; but he answered never a word, and seemed to listen with an ill- contained impatience.

The congressman stated to him, "I'm sorry. I know what I said, but your poll numbers are terrible. I just have to withdraw my endorsement". And then all of a sudden "The Donald" broke out in a great flame of anger, stamping with his foot, brandishing the bottle, and carrying on (as the maid described it) like a madman. The congressman took a step back, with the air of one very much surprised and a trifle hurt; and at that "The Donald" broke out of all bounds and clubbed him to the earth. And next moment, with ape-like fury, he was trampling his victim under foot and hailing down a storm of blows, under which the bones were audibly shattered and the body jumped upon the roadway. At the horror of these sights and sounds, the maid fainted.

It was two o'clock when she came to herself and called the police. The murderer was gone long ago; but there lay his victim in the middle of the lane, incredibly mangled. The stick with which the deed had been done, although it was of some rare and very tough and heavy wood, had broken in the middle under the stress of this insensate cruelty; and one splintered half had rolled in the neighboring gutter — the other, without doubt, had been carried away by the murderer. A purse and a gold watch were found upon the victim: but no cards or papers, except a sealed and stamped envelope, which he had been probably carrying to the post, and which bore the name and address of Mr. Starr.

This was brought to the lawyer the next morning before he was out of bed; and he had no sooner seen it, and been told the circumstances than he shot out a solemn lip. 'I shall say nothing till I have seen the body,' said he; 'this may be very serious. Have the kindness to wait while I dress.' And with the same grave countenance he hurried through his breakfast and drove to the police station, whither the body had been carried. As soon as he came into the cell, he nodded.

'Yes,' said he, 'I recognize him. I am sorry to say that this is Speaker of the House, Paul Ryan'

'Good God, sir,' exclaimed the officer, 'is it possible?' And the next moment his eye lighted up with professional ambition. 'This will make a deal of noise,' he said. 'And perhaps you can help us to the man.' And he briefly narrated what the maid had seen, and showed the broken stick.

Mr. Starr had already quailed at the name of Trump; but when the stick was bottle before him, he could doubt no longer; broken and battered as it was, he recognized it as Trump Vodka.
'Is "The Donald" a person with very small hands?' he inquired.

'Particularly small in hands and other areas that a lady does not mention, and particularly wicked-looking, is what the maid calls him,' said the officer.

Mr. Starr reflected; and then, raising his head, 'If you will come with me in my cab,' he said, 'I think I can take you to his house.'

It was by this time about nine in the morning, and the first fog of the season. A great lowered over heaven, but the wind was continually charging and routing these embattled vapors; so that as the cab crawled from street to street, Mr. Starr beheld a marvelous number of degrees and hues of twilight; for here it would be dark like the back-end of evening; and there would be a glow of a rich, lurid brown, like the light of some strange conflagration; and here, for a moment, the fog would be quite broken up, and a haggard shaft of daylight would glance in between the swirling wreaths. The quarter of trump Tower seen under these changing glimpses, with its gaudy ways, and slatternly residents, and its gold toilets, seemed, in the lawyer's eyes, like some building in a nightmare. The thoughts of his mind, besides, were of the gloomiest dye; and when he glanced at the companion of his drive, he was conscious of some touch of that terror of the law and the law's officers, which may at times assail the most honest.

As the cab drew up before the address indicated, the fog lifted a little and showed him a dingy street, a Trump Bar, a Trump French Restaurant, a Trump golf shop, and Trump Burgers, many undocumented workers huddled in the doorways, and many women of different nationalities in bikinis, and the next moment the fog settled down again upon that part, as brown as umber, and cut him off from his surroundings. This was the home of Hillary Clinton's favorite; of a man who was heir to a Clinton fortune.

An ivory-faced topless girl in a cheerleader's outfit opened the door. She had an evil face, smoothed by hypocrisy; but she was hot and her manners were excellent. Yes, she said, this was "The Donald's", but he was not at home; he had been in that night very late, but had gone away again in less than an hour; there was nothing strange in that; his habits were very irregular, and he was often absent; for instance, it was nearly two months since she had seen him until yesterday.

'Very well, then, we wish to see his rooms,' said the lawyer; and when the woman began to declare it was impossible, 'I had better tell you who this person is,' he added.

'This is Inspector Comey of the FBI.' A flash of odious joy appeared upon the girl's face.

'Ah!' said she, 'he is in trouble! What has he done?

'Mr. Starr and the inspector exchanged glances. 'He doesn't seem a very popular character, but I really only want to create problems for Secretary Clinton. Do you have any emails from her?' observed the the FBI director.

'And now, my good woman, just let me and this gentleman have a look about us.'

In the whole extent of the house, which but for the old woman remained otherwise empty, "The Donald" had only used a couple of rooms; but these were furnished with luxury and poor taste. A closet was filled with pornography; the plate was of gold, a 200-inch plasma TV hung upon the walls, a gift (as Starr supposed) from The Trump Foundation; and the carpets were of many plies. At this moment, however, the rooms bore every mark of having been recently and hurriedly ransacked; clothes lay about the floor, with their pockets inside out; lock-fast drawers stood open; and on the hearth there lay a pile of gray ashes, as though many papers had been burned. From these embers the inspector disinterred the butt-end of a green checkbook, which had resisted the action of the fire; the other half of the stick was found behind the door. This clinched his suspicions, Comey declared himself delighted. A visit to the bank, where several million dollars were found to be lying to the murderer's credit, completed his gratification.

'You may depend on upon it, sir,' he told Mr. Starr: 'I have him in my hand. He must have lost his head, or he would never have left the bottle or, above all, burned the check- book. Why money's life to the man. We have nothing to do but wait for him at the bank, and get out the handbills.'

This last, however, was not so easy of accomplishment; for "The Donald" had numbered few familiars — even the master of the servant-maid had only seen him twice; his family never answered questions. They agreed on one only point, and that was the haunting sense of unexpressed deformity and tiny hands with which the fugitive impressed his beholders.

INCIDENT OF THE EMAIL

IT was late in the afternoon, when Mr. Starr found his way to Secretary Clinton's door, where he was at once admitted by Bill Clinton, and carried down by the kitchen offices and across a yard which had once been a garden, to the building which was indifferently known as the laboratory or the dissecting- rooms. Bill and Hillary had bought the house with finds from Wall Street speeches they had given. It was the first time that the lawyer had been received in that part of his friend's quarters; and he eyed the dingy, windowless structure with curiosity, and gazed round with a distasteful sense of strangeness as he crossed the theatre, once crowded with eager students and now lying gaunt and silent, the tables laden with chemical apparatus, the floor strewn with crates and littered with packing straw, and the light falling dimly through the foggy cupola. At the further end, a flight of stairs mounted to a door covered with red baize, and through this, Mr. Starr was at last received into the Secretary's cabinet. It was a large room, furnished, among other things, with a mirror and a business table, and looking out upon the court by three dusty windows barred with iron. A fire burned in the grate; a lamp was set lighted on the chimney shelf, and there, close up to the warmth, sat Secretary Clinton, looking deadly sick. She did not rise to meet his visitor, but held out a cold hand and bade him welcome in a changed voice.

'And now,' said Mr. Starr, as soon as Bill had left them, 'you have heard the news?'

The Secretary shuddered.' It was on CNN,' he said. 'I heard it in my dining-room.'

'One word,' said the lawyer. 'Ryan was a slippery one, but so are you, and I want to know what I am doing. You have not been mad enough to hide this fellow?'

'Starr, I swear to God, 'cried the Secretary,' I swear to God I will never set eyes on him again. I bind my honor to you that I am done with him in this world. It is all at an end. And indeed he does not want my help; you do not know him as I do; he is safe, he is quite safe; mark my words, he will never more be heard of.'

The lawyer listened gloomily; he did not like his friend's feverish manner. 'You seem pretty sure of him,' said he; 'and for your sake, I hope you may be right. If it came to a trial, your name might appear.'

'I am quite sure of him,' replied Clinton; 'I have grounds for certainty that I cannot share with anyone. But there is one thing on which you may advise me. I have — I have received a letter, and I am at a loss whether I should show it to the police. I should like to leave it in your hands, Starr; you would judge wisely, I am sure; I have so great a trust in you.'

'You fear, I suppose, that it might lead to his detection? 'asked the lawyer.

'No,' said the other.' I cannot say that I care what becomes of Trump; I am quite done with him. I was thinking of my own character, which this hateful business has rather exposed.'

Starr ruminated a while; he was surprised at his friend's selfishness, and yet relieved by it. 'Well,' said he, at last, 'let me see the letter.'

The letter was written in an odd, upright hand and signed 'Donald J. Trump": and it signified, briefly enough, that the writer's benefactor, Secretary Clinton, whom he had long so unworthily repaid for a thousand generosities, need labor under no alarm for his safety, As he had means of escape on which he placed a sure dependence. The lawyer liked this letter well enough; it put a better color on the intimacy than he had looked for, and he blamed himself for some of his past suspicions.

'Have you the envelope?' he asked.

'I burned it,' replied Clinton,' before I thought what I was about. But it bore no postmark. The note was handed in.'

'Shall I keep this and sleep upon it?' asked Starr.

'I wish you to judge for me entirely,' was the reply. 'I have lost confidence in myself.'

'Well, I shall consider,' returned the lawyer. 'And now one word more: it was Trump who dictated the terms in your will about that disappearance?'

The Secretary seemed seized with a qualm of faintness: he shut his mouth tight and nodded.

'I knew it,' said Starr. 'He meant to murder you – or at least ruin your poll numbers. You have had a fine escape.'

'I have had what is far more to the purpose,' returned the Secretary solemnly: 'I have had a lesson — O God, Starr, what a lesson I have had!' And she covered her face for a moment with her hands.

On his way out, the lawyer stopped and had a word or two with Bill. 'By the by,' said he, 'there was a letter handed in to-day: what was the messenger like?' But Bill was positive nothing had come except by post;' and only circulars by that,' he added.

This news sent off the visitor with his fears renewed. Plainly the letter had come by the secret door; possibly, indeed, it had been written in the cabinet; and if that were so, it must be differently judged, and handled with the more caution. The newsboys, as he went, were crying themselves hoarse along the footways: 'Special edition. The shocking murder of a P.R.' That was the funeral oration of one friend and client, and he could not help a certain apprehension lest the good name of another should be sucked down in the eddy of the scandal. It was, at least, a ticklish decision that he had to make; and self- reliant as he was by habit, he began to cherish a longing for advice. It was not to be had directly; but perhaps, he thought, it might be fished for.

Presently after, he sat with Mr. Comey, the FBI Director, and midway between, at a nicely calculated distance from the fire, a bottle of a particular old wine that had long dwelt in the foundations of his house. The fog still slept on the wing above the drowned city, where the lights glimmered like carbuncles; and through the muffle and smother of these fallen clouds, the procession of the town's life was still rolling in through the great arteries with a sound as of a mighty wind. But the room was gay with firelight.

In the bottle the acids were long ago resolved; the imperial dye had softened with time, as the color grows richer in stained windows; and the glow of hot autumn afternoons on hillside vineyards was ready to be set free and to disperse the fogs. Insensibly the lawyer melted. There was no man from whom he kept fewer secrets than Mr. Comey, and he was not always sure that he kept as many as he meant. Guest had often been on business to the doctor's; he knew Bill; he could scarce have failed to hear of "The Donald"'s familiarity about the house; he might draw conclusions: was it not as well, then, that he should see a letter which put that mystery to rights? And above all since Comey, being a great student and critic of handwriting, would consider the step natural and obliging? The Director, besides, was a man of counsel; he would scarce read so strange a document without dropping a remark; and by that remark Mr. Starr might shape his future course.

'This is a sad business about Paul Ryan,' he said.

'Yes, sir, indeed. It has elicited a great deal of public feeling,' returned Comey. 'The man, of course, was mad.'

'I should like to hear your views on that,' replied Starr.

'I have a document here in his handwriting; it is between ourselves, for I scarce know what to do about it; it is an ugly business at the best. But there it is; quite in your way a murderer's autograph.'

Comey's eyes brightened, and he sat down at once and studied it with passion. 'No, sir,' he said: 'not mad; but it is an odd hand.'

'And by all accounts, a very odd writer,' added the lawyer. Just then the servant entered with a note.

'Is that from Secretary Clinton, sir?' inquired the clerk. 'I thought I knew the writing. Anything private, Mr. Starr?'

'Only an invitation to dinner. Why? Do you want to see it?'

'One moment. I thank you, sir"; and the FBI Director laid the two sheets of paper alongside and sedulously compared their contents. 'Thank you, sir,' he said, returning both; 'it's a very interesting autograph.'

There was a pause, during which Mr. Starr struggled with himself. 'Why did you compare them, Comey?' he in- quired suddenly.

'Well, sir,' returned the Director, 'there's a rather singular resemblance; the two hands are in many points identical: only differently sloped.'

'Rather quaint,' said Starr.

'It is, as you say, rather quaint,' returned Comey.

'I wouldn't speak of this note, you know,' said the Starr.

'No, sir,' said the Director. 'I understand.'

But no sooner was Mr. Starr alone that night than he locked the note into his safe, where it reposed from that time forward. 'What!' he thought.' Hillary Clinton forge for a murderer!' And his blood ran cold in his veins.

REMARKABLE INCIDENT OF PRESIDENT OBAMA

TIME ran on; not much was offered in reward, for the death of Paul Ryan really was not resented that greatly as a no one truly had any affection for the man. Still it was a murder and "The Donald" had disappeared out of the ken of the police as though he had never existed. Much of his past was unearthed, indeed, and all disreputable: tales came out of the man's cruelty, at once so callous and violent; of his vile life, of his strange associates, of the hatred that seemed to have surrounded his career; but of his present whereabouts, not a whisper. Still, since this was considered the work of the "dishonest media" no really cared.

From the time he had left the house on the morning of the murder, he was simply blotted out; and gradually, as time drew on, Mr. Starr began to recover from the hotness of his alarm, and to grow more at quiet with himself. The death of Paul Ryan was, to his way of thinking, more than paid for by the disappearance of "The Donald". Now that that evil influence had been withdrawn, a new life began for Secretary Clinton. She came out of her seclusion, renewed relations with her friends, became once more their familiar guest and entertainer; and whilst she had always been, known for charities, she was now no less distinguished for religion. She was busy, she was much in the open air, she did well; her face seemed to open and brighten, as if with an inward consciousness of service; and for more than two months, the Secretary was at peace.

On the 8th of January, Starr had dined at the Secretary's with a small party; Obama had been there, and the face of the host had looked from one to the other as in the old days when the trio were inseparable friends. On the 12th, and again on the 14th, the door was shut against the lawyer. 'The Secretary was confined to the house,' Bill said, 'and saw no one.' On the 15th, he tried again, and was again refused; and having now been used for the last two months to see his friend almost daily, he found this return of solitude to weigh upon his spirits. The fifth night he had in Guest to dine with him, and the sixth he betook himself to President Obama's.

There at least he was not denied admittance; but when he came in, he was shocked at the change which had taken place in the President's appearance. He had his death-warrant written legibly upon his face. His flesh had fallen away; he was visibly grayer and older; and yet it was not so much, these tokens of a swift physical decay that arrested the lawyer's notice, as a look in the eye and quality of manner that seemed to testify to some deep-seated terror of the mind. It was unlikely that the doctor should fear death, and yet that was what Starr was tempted to suspect. 'Yes,' he thought; 'he is a doctor, he must know his own state and that his days are counted; and the knowledge is more than he can bear.' And yet when Starr remarked on his ill-looks, it was with an air of greatness that Obama declared himself a doomed man. 'I have had a shock,' he said, 'and I shall never recover. It is a question of weeks. Well, life has been pleasant; I liked it; yes, sir, I used to like it. I sometimes think if we knew all, we should be gladder to get away.'

'Clinton is ill, too,' observed Starr. 'Have you

seen him?'

But Obama's face changed, and he held up a trembling hand. 'I wish to see or hear no more of Secretary Clinton,' he said in a loud, unsteady voice. 'I am quite done with that person, and I beg that you will spare me any allusion to one whom I regard as dead.'

'Tut-tut,' said Mr. Starr; and then after a considerable pause,' Can't I do anything?' he inquired. 'We are three very old friends, Obama; we shall not live to make others.'

'Nothing can be done,' returned Obama; 'ask her.' She will not see me,' said the lawyer.

'I am not surprised at that,' was the reply. 'Some day, Starr, after I am dead, you may perhaps come to learn the right and wrong of this. I cannot tell you. And in the meantime, if you can sit and talk with me about other things, for God's sake, stay and do so; but if you cannot keep clear of this accursed topic, then, in God's name, go, for I cannot bear it.'

As soon as he got home, Starr sat down and wrote to Clinton, complaining of his exclusion from the house, and asking the cause of this unhappy break with Obama; and the next day brought him a long answer, often very pathetically worded, and sometimes darkly mysterious in drift.

The quarrel with Obama was incurable. 'I do not blame our old friend,' Clinton wrote, 'but I share his view that we must never meet. I mean from henceforth to lead a life of extreme seclusion; you must not be surprised, nor must you doubt my friendship, if my door is often shut even to you. You must suffer me to go my own dark way. I have brought on myself a punishment and a danger that I cannot name. If I am the chief of sinners, I am the chief of sufferers also. I could not think that this earth contained a place for sufferings and terrors so unbelievable, and you can do but one thing, Starr, to lighten this destiny, and that is to respect my silence.' Starr was amazed; the dark influence of Trump had been withdrawn, the Secretary had returned to his old tasks and amenities; a week ago, the prospect had smiled with every promise of a cheerful and an honored age; and now in a moment, friendship, and peace of mind, and the whole tenor of his life were wrecked. So great and unprepared a change pointed to madness; but in view of Obama's manner and words, there must lie for it some deeper ground.

A week afterward President Obama took to golfing, and in something less than a fortnight he was on a golfing vacation. Starr had been sadly affected and locked the door of his business room, and sitting there by the light of a melancholy candle, drew out and set before him an envelope addressed by the hand and sealed with the seal of his dead friend. 'PRIVATE: for the hands of K. Starr ALONE and in the the case of his predecease to be destroyed unread,' so it was emphatically scribed; and the lawyer dreaded to behold the contents. 'I have lost one friend to-day,' he thought: 'what if this should cost me another?' And then he condemned the fear as a disloyalty and broke the seal. Within there was another enclosure, likewise sealed, and marked upon the cover as 'not to be opened till the death or disappearance of Secretary Hillary Clinton.' Starr could not trust his eyes. Yes, it was disappearance; here again, as in the mad will which he had long ago restored to its author, here again, were the idea of a disappearance and the name of Hillary Clinton bracketed. But in the will that idea had sprung from the sinister suggestion of the man Trump; it was set there with a purpose all too plain and horrible. Written by the hand of Obama, what should it mean? A great curiosity came on the trustee, to disregard the prohibition and dive at once to the bottom of these mysteries; but professional honor and faith to his golfing friend were stringent obligations, and the packet slept in the inmost corner of his private safe.

It is one thing to mortify curiosity, another to conquer it; and it may be doubted if, from that day forth, Starr desired the society of Secretary

Clinton with the same eagerness. He thought of her kindly, but his thoughts were disquieted and fearful. He went to call indeed, but he was perhaps relieved to be denied admittance; perhaps, in his heart, he preferred to speak with Bill upon the doorstep and surrounded by the air and sounds of the open city, rather than to be admitted into that house of voluntary bondage, and to sit and speak with its inscrutable recluse. Bill had, indeed, no very pleasant news to communicate. The Secretary, it appeared, now more than ever confined herself to the cabinet over the office, where she would sometimes even sleep; she was out of spirits, she had grown very silent, she did not read; it seemed as if she had something on her mind. Starr became so used to the unvarying character of these reports that he fell off little by little in the frequency of his visits.

INCIDENT AT THE WINDOW

It chanced on Sunday, when Mr. Starr was on his usual walk with Reince Priebus, that their way lay once again through the by-street; and that when they came in front of the door, both stopped to gaze on it.

'Well,' said Priebus, 'that story's at an end at least. We shall never see more of "The Donald".'

'I hope not,' said Starr. 'Did I ever tell you that I once saw him, and shared your feeling of repulsion?'

'It was impossible to do the one without the

other,' returned Priebus. "To think he was our nominee. And by the way, what an ass you must have thought me, not to know that this was a back way to Secretary Clinton's! All of the donors she and Bill entertained came in through this door. It was partly your own fault that I found it out, even when I did.'

'So you found it out, did you?' said Starr. 'But if that be so, we may step into the court and take a look at the windows. To tell you the truth, I am uneasy about poor Clinton; and even outside, I feel as if the presence of a friend might do her good.'

The court was very cool and a little damp, and full of premature twilight, although the sky, high up overhead, was still bright with sunset. The middle one of the three windows was half-way open; and sitting close beside it, taking the air with an infinite sadness of mien, like some disconsolate prisoner, Starr saw Secretary Clinton.

'What! Clinton!' he cried. 'I trust you are better.'

'I am very low, Starr,' replied the Secretary, drearily.

'Very low. It will not last long, thank God.'

'You stay too much indoors,' said the lawyer. 'You should be out, whipping up the base like Reince Priebus and me. Come, now; get your hat and take a quick turn with us.'

'You are very good,' sighed the other. 'I should like to very much; but no, no, no, it is quite impossible; I dare not. But indeed, Starr, I am very glad to see you; this is really a great pleasure; I would ask you and Reince Priebus up, but the place is really not fit and I hate most Republicans.'

'Why then,' said the lawyer, good-naturedly, 'the best thing we can do is to stay down here and speak with you from where we are.'

'That is just what I was about to venture to propose,' returned the Secretary with a smile. But the words were hardly uttered before the smile was struck out of her face and succeeded by an expression of such abject terror and despair, as froze the very blood of the two gentlemen below. They saw it but for a glimpse, for the window was instantly thrust down; but that glimpse had been sufficient, and they turned and left the court without a word. In silence, too, they traversed the by-street; and it was not until they had come into a neighboring thoroughfare, where even upon a Sunday there were still some stirrings of life, that Mr. Starr at last turned and looked at his companion. They were both pale, and there was an answering horror in their eyes.

'May God forgive us,' said Mr. Starr.

But Reince Priebus only nodded his head very seriously and walked on once more in silence.

The Last Night

MR. STARR was sitting by his fireside one
evening after dinner when he was surprised to

receive a visit from Bill.

'Bless me, Bill, what brings you here?' he cried; and then taking a second look at him, 'What ails you?' he added; 'is the Secretary ill?'

'Mr. Starr,' said the man,' there is something wrong.' Take a seat, and here is a glass of wine for you,' said the lawyer. 'Now, take your time, and tell me plainly what you want.'

'You know the Secretary's ways, sir,' replied Bill, 'and how she shuts herself up. Well, she's shut up again in the cabinet; and I don't like it, sir I wish I may die if I like it. Mr. Starr, sir, I'm afraid.'

'Now, my good man,' said the lawyer, 'be explicit. What are you afraid of?'

'I've been afraid for about a week,' returned Bill, doggedly disregarding the question, 'and I can bear it no more. 'The man's appearance amply bore out his words; his manner was altered for the worse; and except for the moment when he had first announced his terror, he had not once looked the lawyer in the face. Even now, he sat with the glass of wine untasted on his knee, and his eyes directed to a corner of the floor. 'I can bear it no more,' he repeated.

'Come,' said the lawyer, 'I see you have some good reason, Bill; I see there is something seriously amiss. Try to tell me what it is.'

'I think there's been foul play,' said Bill, hoarsely.

'Foul play!' cried the lawyer, a good deal frightened and rather inclined to be irritated in consequence. 'What foul play? What does the man mean? Is it perjury?'

'I daren't say, sir' was the answer; 'but will you come along with me and see for yourself?'

Mr. Starr's only answer was to rise and get his hat and great-coat; but he observed with wonder the greatness of the relief that appeared upon the butler's face, and perhaps with no less, that the wine was still untasted when he set it down to follow.

It was a wild, cold, seasonable night of March, with a pale moon, lying on her back as though the wind had tilted her, and a flying wrack of the most diaphanous and lawny texture. The wind made talking difficult and flecked the blood into the face. It seemed to have swept the streets unusually bare of passengers, besides; for Mr. Starr thought he had never seen that part of the city so deserted. He could have wished it otherwise; never in his life had he been conscious of so sharp a wish to see and touch his fellow-creatures; for struggle as he might, there was borne in upon his mind a crushing anticipation of calamity. The square, when they got there, was all full of wind and dust, and the thin trees in the garden were lashing themselves along the railing. Bill, who had kept all the way a pace or two ahead, now pulled up in the middle of the pavement, and in spite of the biting weather, took off his hat and mopped his brow with a red pocket-handkerchief. But for all his hurry, these were not the dews of exertion that he wiped away, but the moisture of some strangling anguish; for his face was white and his voice, when he spoke, harsh and broken.

'Well, sir,' he said, 'here we are, and God grant there be nothing wrong.'

'Amen, Bill,' said the lawyer.

Thereupon the servant knocked in a very guarded manner; the door was opened on the chain, and a voice asked from within, 'Is that you, Bill?'

'It's all right,' said Bill. 'Open the door.' The hall, when they entered it, was brightly lighted up; the fire was built high; and about it the many lobbyists, wall street brokers, and politicians stood huddled together like a flock of sheep. At the sight of Mr. Starr, one lobbyist broke into hysterical whimpering; and a broker, crying out, 'Bless God! It's Mr. Starr,' ran forward as if to take him in her arms.

'What, what? Are you all here?' said the lawyer peevishly.

'Very irregular, very unseemly; your wife would be far from pleased.'

'They're all afraid,' said Bill.

Blank silence followed, no one protesting; only

the lobbyist lifted up her voice and now wept loudly.

'Hold your tongue!' Bill said to her, with a ferocity of accent that testified to his own jangled nerves; and indeed, when the girl had so suddenly raised the note of her lamentation, they had all started and turned toward the inner door with faces of dreadful expectation. 'And now,' continued Bill, addressing the other, 'reach me a flashlight, and we'll get this through hands at once.' And then he begged Mr. Starr to follow him and led the way to the back-garden.

'Now, sir,' said he, 'you come as gently as you can. I want you to hear, and I don't want you to be heard. And see here, sir, if by any chance he was to ask you in, don't go.'

Mr. Starr's nerves, at this unlooked-for termination, gave a jerk that nearly threw him from his balance; but he recollected his courage and followed Bill into the building and through the many rooms, with its lumber of crates and bottles, to the foot of the stair. Here Bill motioned him to stand on one side and listen; while he himself, setting down the falshlight and making a great and obvious call on his resolution, mounted the steps and knocked with a somewhat uncertain hand on the handle of the cabinet door.

'Tt's Mr. Starr, honey, asking to see you, 'he called; and even as he did so, once more violently signed to the lawyer to give ear.

A voice answered from within: 'Tell him I cannot see anyone,' it said complainingly.

'Thank you, honey,' said Bill, with a note of something like triumph in his voice; and taking up his candle, he led Mr. Starr back across the yard and into the great kitchen, where the fire was out and the beetles were leaping on the floor.

'Sir,' he said, looking Mr. Starr in the eyes,' was that my wife's voice?'

'It seems much changed,' replied the lawyer, very pale, but giving look for look.

'Changed? Well, yes, I think so,' said Bill. 'Have I been years in this woman's house, to be deceived about his voice? No, sir; she's made away with; she was made, away with eight days ago, when we heard her cry out upon the name of God; and who's in there instead of him, and why it stays there, is a thing that cries to Heaven, Mr. Starr!'

'This is a very strange tale, Bill; this is rather a wild tale, my man,' said Mr. Starr, biting his finger. 'Suppose it were as you suppose, supposing Secretary Clinton to have been — well, murdered, what could induce the murderer to stay? That won't hold water; it doesn't commend itself to reason.'

'Well, Mr. Starr, you are a hard man to satisfy, but I'll do it yet,' said Bill. 'All this last week (you must know) him, or it, or whatever it is that lives in that cabinet, has been crying night and day for some sort of medicine and cannot get it to his mind. It was sometimes her way — Secretary Clinton, that is — to write her orders on a sheet of paper and throw it on the stair. We've had nothing else this week back; nothing but papers, and a closed door, and the very meals left there to be smuggled in when nobody was looking. Well, sir, every day, ay, and twice and thrice in the same day, there have been orders and complaints, and I have been sent flying to all the CIA scientists in town. Every time I brought the stuff back, there would be another paper telling me to return it, because it was not pure, and another order to a different firm. This drug is wanted bitter bad, sir, whatever for.'

'Have you any of these papers?' asked Mr. Starr. Bill felt in his pocket and handed out a crumpled note, which the lawyer, bending nearer to the candle, carefully examined. Its contents ran thus:

'Secretary Clinton presents her compliments. She assures them that their last sample is impure and quite useless for her present purpose. In the year 2016, Secretary C. purchased a somewhat large quantity. She now begs them to search with the most sedulous care and should any of the same quality be left, to forward it to him at once. The expense is no consideration. The importance of this to Secretary C. can hardly be exaggerated.' So far the letter had run composedly enough, but here with a sudden splutter of the pen, the writer's emotion had broken loose. 'For God's sake,' he had added, 'find me some of the old.'

'This is a strange note,' said Mr. Starr; and then sharply, 'How do you come to have it open?'

'The agent was main angry, sir, and he threw it back to me like so much dirt,' returned Bill.
'This is unquestionably the Secretary's hand, do you know?' resumed the lawyer.

'I thought it looked like it,' said Bill rather sulkily; and then, with another voice, 'But what does it matter? 'He said. 'I've seen her!'

'Seen her?' repeated Mr. Starr. 'Well?'

'That's it!' said Bill. 'It was this way. I came suddenly into the theater from the garden. It seems she had slipped out to look for this drug or whatever it is; for the cabinet door was open, and there she was at the far end of the room digging among the crates. She looked up when I came in, gave a kind of cry, and whipped up-stairs into the cabinet. It was but for one minute that I saw her, but the hair stood upon my head like quills. Sir, if that was my wife, why had she a Trump mask upon her face? If it was her, why did she cry out like a rat, and run from me? I have served her long enough. And then...' The man paused and passed his hand over his face.

'These are all very strange circumstances,' said Mr. Starr, 'but I think I begin to see daylight. Your wife, Bill, is plainly seized with one of those maladies that both torture and deform the sufferer; hence, for aught I know, the alteration of her voice; hence the mask and the avoidance of her friends; hence her eagerness to find this drug, by means of which the poor soul retains some hope of ultimate recovery — God grant that she be not deceived! There is my explanation; it is sad enough, Bill, ay, and appalling to consider; but it is plain and natural, hangs well together, and delivers us from all exorbitant alarms.'

'Sir,' said the butler, turning to a sort of mottled pallor, 'That thing was not my wife, and there's the truth. My wife' here he looked round him and began to whisper —is a fine build of a woman, and this was more of a fat small handed troll.'

Starr attempted to protest. 'O, sir,' cried Bill, 'do you think I do not know my wife after many years? Do you think I do not know where his head comes to in the cabinet door, where I saw him every morning of my life? No, Sir, that thing in the mask was never Secretary Clinton — God knows what it was, but it was never Secretary Clinton; and it is the belief of my heart that there was murder done.'

'Bill,' replied the lawyer, 'if you say that, it will become my duty to make certain. Much as I desire to consider your master's feelings, much as I am puzzled by this note which seems to prove him to be still alive, I shall consider it my duty to break through that door.'

Ah, Mr. Starr, that's talking!' cried the butler.

'And now comes the second question,' resumed Starr: 'Who is going to do it?'

'Why, you and me,' was the undaunted reply.

'That's very well said,' returned the lawyer; 'and what- ever comes of it, I shall make it my business to see you are no loser.'

'There is an ax in the theater, continued Bill; 'and you might take the kitchen poker for yourself.'

The lawyer took that rude but weighty instrument into his hand and balanced it. 'Do you know, Bill,' he said, looking up, 'that you and I are about to place ourselves in a position of some peril?'

'You may say so, sir, indeed,' returned the former President.

'It is well, then, that we should be frank,' said the other.

'We both think more than we have said; let us make a clean breast. This masked figure that you saw, did you recognize it?'

'Well, sir, it went so quick, and the creature was so doubled up, that I could hardly swear to that,' was the answer.

'But if you mean, was it "The Donald"? —

Why, yes, I think it was! You see, it was much of the same smallness; and it had the same quick, arrogant way with it; and then who else could have got in by the donor door? You have not forgotten, sir that at the time of the murder he had still the key with him? But that's not all. I don't know, Mr. Starr, if ever you met this "The Donald"?'

'Yes,' said the lawyer, 'I once spoke with him.'

'Then you must know as well as the rest of us that there was something queer about that gentleman — something that gave a man a turn — I don't know rightly how to say it, sir, beyond this: that you felt it in your marrow kind of cold and thin.'

'I own I felt something of what you describe,' said Mr. Starr.

'Quite so, sir,' returned Bill. 'Well, when that masked thing like a monkey jumped from among the chemicals and whipped into the cabinet, it went down my spine like ice. Oh, I know it's not evidence, Mr. Starr. I'm book-learned enough for that; but a man has his, feelings, and I give you my Bible-word it was "The Donald"!'

'Ay, ay,' said the lawyer. 'My fears incline to the same point. Evil, I fear, founded — evil was sure to come — of that connection. Ay, truly, I believe you; I believe poor Hillary is killed; and I believe his murderer (for what purpose, God alone can tell) is still lurking in his victim's room. Well, let our name be vengeance. Call Senecal.'

The butler came at the summons, very white and nervous.

Pull yourself together, Senecal,' said the lawyer. 'This suspense, I know, is telling upon all of you; but it is now our intention to make an end of it. Bill, here, and I are going to force our way into the cabinet. If all is well, my shoulders are broad enough to bear the blame. Meanwhile, lest anything should really be amiss, or any malefactor seeks to escape by the back, you and the boy must go round the corner with a pair of good sticks and take your post at the laboratory door. We give you ten minutes to get to your stations.'

As Senecal left, the lawyer looked at his watch. 'And now, Bill, let us get to ours,' he said; and taking the poker under his arm, led the way into the yard. The scud had banked over the moon, and it was now quite dark. The wind, which only broke in puffs and draughts into that deep well of the building, tossed the light of the candle to and fro about their steps until they came into the shelter of the theater, where they sat down silently to wait. The city hummed solemnly all around; but nearer at hand, the stillness was only broken by the sounds of a footfall moving to and fro along the cabinet floor.

'So it will walk all day, Sir,' whispered Bill; 'and the better part of the night. Only when a new sample comes from the CIA, there's a bit of a break. Ah, it's an ill conscience that's such an enemy to rest! Ah, sir, there's blood foully shed in every step of it! But hark again a little closer — put your heart in your ears, Mr. Starr, and tell me, is that the Secretary's foot?'

The steps fell heavily and oddly, with a certain swing, for all they went so slowly; it was different indeed from the light tread of Hillary Clinton. Starr sighed. 'Is there never anything else?' he asked.

Bill nodded. 'Once,' he said. 'Once I heard it weeping!'

'Weeping? How that?' said the lawyer, conscious of a sudden chill of horror.

'Weeping like her poll numbers dropped 10 points or a lost soul,' said Bill. 'I came away with that upon my heart that I could have wept too.'

But now the ten minutes drew to an end. Bill disinterred the ax from under a stack of packing straw; the flashlight was set upon the nearest table to light them to the attack; and they drew near with bated breath to where that patient foot was still going up and down, up and down, in the quiet of the night.

'Clinton,' cried Starr, with a loud voice, 'I demand to see you.' He paused a moment, but there came no reply. 'I give you fair warning, our suspicions are aroused, and I must and shall see you,' he resumed; 'if not by fair means, then by foul! If not of your consent, then by brute force!'

'Starr,' said the voice, 'Get lost, loser!' Ah, that's not Clinton's voice — it's Trump's!' cried Starr.

'Down with the door, Bill!'

Bill swung the ax over his shoulder; the blow shook the building, and the red door leaped against the lock and hinges. A dismal screech, as of mere animal terror, rang from the cabinet. Up went the axe again, and again the panels crashed and the frame bounded; four times the blow fell; but the wood was tough and the fittings were of excellent workmanship; and it was not until the fifth, that the lock burst in sunder and the wreck of the door fell inwards on the carpet.

The besiegers, appalled by their own riot and the stillness that had succeeded, stood back a little and peered in. There lay the cabinet before their eyes in the quiet lamplight, a good fire glowing and chattering on the hearth, the kettle singing its thin strain, a drawer or two open, papers neatly set forth on the table, and nearer the fire, the things laid out for tea: the quietest room, you would have said, and, but for the bottles full of chemicals, the most commonplace that night in the city.

Right in the midst there lay the body of a man

sorely contorted and still twitching. They drew near on tiptoe, turned it on its back and beheld the face of Donald Trump. He was dressed in a smart pantsuit far too small for him, and a frilled blouse of the Secretary's; the cords of his face twitched and he mumbled somewhat incoherently, "I'm the best. I have the best plans, the best words, the best hair…" and by the crushed vial in the hand and the strong smell of kernels that hung upon the air - and the woman's clothes he was wearing; he hoped the Trumps candidacy was over, but doubted any of this would really bother his followers.

'We have come too late,' he said sternly, 'whether to save or punish. Trump is likely to become President, and it only remains for us to find your wife.'

The far greater proportion of the building was occupied by the theater, which filled almost the whole ground story and was lighted from above, and by the cabinet, which formed an upper story at one end and looked upon the court. A corridor joined the theater to the door on the street, and with this, the cabinet communicated separately by the second flight of stairs. There were a few dark closets and a spacious cellar. All these they now thoroughly examined. Each closet needed but a glance, for they were empty, and all, by the dust that fell from their doors, had stood long unopened. The cellar, indeed, was filled with sex toys, mostly dating from the times of the wild parties Bill threw for his "interns", but even as they opened the door they were advertised of the uselessness of further search, by the fall of a perfect mat of cobweb which had for years sealed up the entrance. Nowhere was there any trace of Hillary Clinton, dead or alive.

Bill stamped on the flags of the corridor. 'She must be buried here,' he said, hearkening to the sound.

'Or she may have fled,' said Starr, and he turned to examine the door in the by-street. It was locked; and lying nearby on the flags, they found the key, already stained with rust.

'This does not look like use,' observed the lawyer.

'Use!' echoed Bill. 'Do you not see, sir, it is broken? Much as if a man had stamped on it.'

'Ay,' continued Starr,' and the fractures, too, are rusty.' The two men looked at each. 'This is beyond me, Bill,' said the lawyer. 'Let us go back to the cabinet.' They mounted the stair in silence, and still with an occasional awestruck glance at the dead body, proceeded more thoroughly to examine the contents of the cabinet. At one table, there were traces of chemical work, various measured heaps of some white salt being laid on glass saucers, as though for an experiment in which the unhappy man had been prevented.

'That is the same drug that I was always bringing him,' said Bill; and even as he spoke, the kettle with a startling noise boiled over.

This brought them to the fireside, where the easy-chair was drawn cozily up, and the teething's stood ready to the sitter's elbow, the very sugar in the cup. There were several books on a shelf; one lay beside the tea-things open, and Starr was amazed to find it a copy of a pious work, for which Clinton had several times expressed a great esteem, annotated, in her own hand, with startling blasphemies.

Next, in the course of their review of the chamber, the searchers came to the cheval glass, into whose depths they looked with an involuntary horror. But it was so turned as to show them nothing but the rosy glow playing on the roof, the fire sparkling in a hundred repetitions along the glazed front of the presses, and their own pale and fearful countenances stooping to look in.

'This mirror has seen some strange things, sir,' whispered Bill.

'Knowing you Bill, I am sure of that. And surely none stranger than itself,' echoed the lawyer in the same tones. 'For what did Clinton' — he caught himself up at the word with a start, and then conquering the weakness — 'what could Clinton want with it?' he said.

'You may say that!' said Bill. Next, they turned to the table. On the desk among the neat array of papers, a large envelope was uppermost, and bore, in the Secretary's hand, the name of Mr. Starr. The lawyer unsealed it, and several enclosures fell to the floor. The first was a will, drawn in the same eccentric terms as the one which he had returned six months before, to serve as a testament in case of death and as a deed of gift in case of disappearance; but, in place of the name of Donald Trump, the lawyer, with indescribable amazement, read the name of Ken Starr. He looked at Bill, and then back at the paper, and last of all at the orange colored malefactor tweeting in the corner.

'My head goes round,' he said. 'He has been all these days in possession; he had no cause to like me; he must have raged to see himself displaced, and he has not destroyed this document.'

He caught up the next paper; it was a brief note in the Secretary's hand and dated at the top.

'O Bill!' the lawyer cried, 'she was alive and here this day. She cannot have been disposed of in so short a space, she must be still alive, she must have fled! And then, why fled? And how? And in that case, can we venture to declare this suicide? Oh, we must be careful. I foresee that we may yet involve your wife in some dire catastrophe.'

'Why don't you read it, sir?' asked Bill.

'Because I fear,' replied the lawyer solemnly. 'God grant I have no cause for it!' And with that he brought the paper to his eyes and read as follows:

'MY DEAR STARR, — When this shall fall into your hands, I shall have disappeared, under what circumstances I have not the penetration to foresee, but my instinct and all the circumstances of my nameless situation tell me that the end is sure and must be early. Go then, and first read the narrative which Obama warned me he was to place in your hands; and if you care to hear more, turn to the confession of

Your unworthy and unhappy friend, Hillary Clinton.'

'There was a third enclosure?' asked Starr.

'Here, sir,' said Bill, and gave into his hands a considerable packet sealed in several places.

The lawyer put it in his pocket. 'I would say nothing of this paper. If your wife has fled or is dead, we may at least save her credit. It is now ten; I must go home and read these documents in quiet, but I shall be back before midnight when we shall send for the police.'

They went out, locking the door of the theater behind them; and Starr, once more leaving the servants gathered about the fire in the hall, trudged back to his office to read the two narratives in which this mystery was now to be explained.

PRESIDENT OBAMA'S NARRATIVE

ON the ninth of January, now four days ago, I received by the evening delivery a registered envelope, addressed in the hand of my colleague and old companion, Hillary Clinton. I was a good deal surprised by this; for we were by no means in the habit of correspondence; I had seen the woman, dined with her, indeed, the night before; and I could imagine nothing in our intercourse that should justify formality of registration. The contents increased my wonder; for this is how the letter ran:

'10th December 1016

'MY DEAR OBAMA, You are one of my oldest friends; and although we may have differed at times on whether you know what you are doing, I cannot remember, at least on my side, any break in our affection. There was never a day when, if you had said to me, 'Clinton, my life, my honor, my reason, depend on upon you,' I would not have sacrificed Bill's wandering "jewels" to help you. Obama, my life, my honor my reason, are all at your mercy; if you fail me to-night I am lost. You might suppose, after this preface, that I am going to ask you for something dishonorable to grant. Well it is me, but judge for yourself.

'I want you to postpone all other engagements for tonight — ay, even if you were summoned to the bedside of an emperor; to take an Air Force One; and with this email in your Blackberry for consultation, to have your motorcade drive straight to my house. Bill, my butler, has his orders; you will find, him waiting for your arrival with a locksmith. The door of my cabinet is then to be forced: and you are to go in alone; to open the glazed press (letter E) on the left hand, breaking the lock if it be shut; and to draw out, with all its contents as they stand, the fourth drawer from the top or (which is the same thing) the third from the bottom. In my extreme distress of mind, I have a morbid fear of misdirecting you; but even if I am in error, you may know the right drawer by its contents: some powders, a vial, and Bill's old little black book. This drawer I beg of you to carry back with you exactly as it stands.

'That is the first part of the service: now for the second. You should be back, if you set out at once on the receipt of this, long before midnight; but I will leave you that amount of margin, not only in the fear of one of those obstacles that can neither be prevented nor foreseen but because an hour when Michelle is in bed is to be preferred for what will then remain to do. At midnight, then, I have to ask you to be alone in the Oval Office, to admit with your own hand a man with orange skin and small hands who will present himself in my name, and to place in his hands the drawer that you will have brought with you from my cabinet. Then you will have played your part and earned my gratitude completely. Five minutes afterward, if you insist upon an explanation, you will have understood that these arrangements are of capital importance; and that by the neglect of one of them, fantastic as they must appear, you might have charged your conscience with my losing the election.

'Confident as I am that you will not trifle with this appeal, my heart sinks and my hand trembles at the bare thought of such a possibility. Think of me at this hour, in a strange place, laboring under a blackness of distress that no fancy can exaggerate, and yet well aware that, if you will but punctually serve me, my troubles will roll away like a story that is told. Serve me, my dear Obama, and save your friend, H. C.'

'P. S. I had already sealed this up when a fresh terror struck upon my soul. It is possible that my personal email server may fail me yet again, and this email does not come into your hands until tomorrow morning. In that case, dear Obama, do my errand when it shall be most convenient for you in the course of the day; and once more expect my messenger at midnight. It may then already be too late; and if that night passes without event, you will know that you have seen the last of Hillary Clinton.'

Upon the reading of this letter, I made sure my colleague was insane; but till that was proved beyond the possibility of doubt, I felt bound to do as she requested. The less I understood of this farrago, the less I was in a position to judge of its importance; and an appeal so worded could not be set aside without a grave responsibility. I rose accordingly from the table, got into Air Force One, landed, and had my motorcade drive straight to Clinton's house. The butler was awaiting my arrival; he had received by the same email as mine and had sent at once for a locksmith and a carpenter. The tradesmen came while we were yet speaking; and we moved to Clinton's old secret donor room, from which (as you are doubtless aware) Clinton's private cabinet is most conveniently entered.

The door was very strong, the lock excellent; the carpenter avowed he would have great trouble and have to do much damage if force were to be used, and the locksmith was near despair. But this last was a handy fellow, and after two hours' work, the door stood open. The press marked E was unlocked; and I took out the drawer, had it filled up with straw and tied in a sheet, and returned with it.

Here I proceeded to examine its contents. The powders were neatly enough made up, but not with the nicety of the dispensing chemist; so that it was plain they were of secret government manufacture; and when I opened one of the wrappers I found what a simple crystalline salt of a white color seemed to me. The vial, to which I next turned my attention, might have been about half-full of a blood-red liquor, which was highly pungent to the sense of smell and seemed to me to contain phosphorus and some volatile ether. At the other ingredients, I could make no guess.

The book was an ordinary version-book and contained little but a series of dates. These covered a period of many years, but I observed that the entries ceased nearly a year ago and quite abruptly. Here and there a brief remark was appended to a date, usually no more than a single word: 'double' occurring perhaps six times in a total of several hundred entries; and once very early in the list and followed by several marks of exclamation, 'total failure!!!' All this, though it whetted my curiosity, told me little that was definite. Here were a vial of some tincture, a paper of some salt, and the record of a series of experiments that had led (like too many of Clinton's investigations) to no end of practical usefulness. How could the presence of these articles in this house affect either the honor, the sanity, or the election prospects of my flighty colleague? If her messenger could go to one place, why could he not go to another? And even granting some impediment, why was this gentleman to be received by me in the Oval Office? The more I reflected the more convinced I grew that the Alt-Right was correct and I was dealing with a case of cerebral disease: and though I dismissed the secret service, I loaded an old revolver, that I might be found in some posture of pretending to support the Second Amendment.

Twelve o'clock had scarce rung out over Washington, ere the knocker sounded very gently on the door. I went myself at the summons and found a large obnoxious man with small hands crouching against the pillars of the portico.

'Have you come from Secretary Clinton?' I asked.

He told me 'yes' by a constrained gesture; and when I had bidden him enter, he did not obey me without a searching backward glance into the darkness of the square. There was a reporter not far off, advancing with his bull's eye open; and at the sight, I thought my visitor started and made greater haste.

These particulars struck me, I confess, disagreeably; and as I followed him into the bright light of the Oval Office, I kept my hand ready on my weapon. Here, at last, I had a chance of clearly seeing him. He had small hands, as I have said; I was struck besides with the shocking expression of his face, with his remarkable combination of swinging arms, orange skin punctuated by white circles around his eyes, a great unruly shock of hair (which appeared to be an ill-fated attempt at a comb-over), and — last but not least — with the odd, subjective disturbance caused by his neighborhood. This bore some resemblance to incipient rigor and was accompanied by a marked sinking of the pulse. At the time, I set it down to some idiosyncratic, personal distaste, and merely wondered at the acuteness of the symptoms; but I have since had reason to believe the cause to lie much deeper in the nature of man, and to turn on some nobler hinge than the principle of hatred.

This person (who had thus, from the first moment of his entrance, struck in me what I can only describe as a disgustful curiosity) was dressed in a fashion that would have made an ordinary person laughable; his clothes, that is to say, although they were of rich and sober fabric, were too tight for him in every measurement — the waist bulging from the above a women's skirt, the waist of the coat above his haunches, and the collar of his blouse strangling his thick neck. Strange to relate, this ludicrous accouterment was far from moving me to laughter. Rather, as there was something abnormal and misbegotten in the very essence of the creature that now faced me — something seizing, surprising, and revolting — this fresh disparity seemed but to fit in with and to reinforce it; so that to my interest in the man's nature and character, there was added a curiosity as to his origin, his life, his fortune and status in the world.

These observations, though they have taken so great a space to be set down in, were yet the work of a few seconds. My visitor was, indeed, on fire with somber excitement.

'Have you got it?' he cried. 'Have you got it?' And so lively was his impatience that he even laid his hand upon my arm and sought to shake me.

I put him back, conscious at his touch of a certain icy pang along my blood. 'Come, sir,' said I. 'You forget that you are germ-a-phobic and hate touching people – particularly minorities. Be seated, if you please.' And I showed him an example, and sat down myself in my customary seat and with as fair an imitation of my ordinary manner to a visitor, as the lateness of the hour, the nature of my preoccupations, and the horror I had of my visitor, would suffer me to muster.

'I beg your pardon, loser,' he replied typically enough.

'What you say is very well founded, and my impatience has shown its heels to my politeness. I come here at the instance of your colleague, Secretary Hillary Clinton, on a piece of business of some moment; and I understood...' He paused and put his hand to his throat, and I could see, in spite of his collected manner that he was wrestling against the approaches of the hysteria — 'I understood, a drawer.'

But here I took pity on my visitor's suspense, and some perhaps on my own growing curiosity. 'There it is, sir,' said I, pointing to the drawer, where it lay on the floor behind a table and still covered with the sheet.

He sprang to it, and then paused, and laid his hand upon his heart: I could hear his teeth grate with the convulsive action of his jaws, and his face was so ghastly to see that I grew alarmed both for his life and reason.

'Compose yourself,' said I.

He turned a dreadful smile to me, and as if with the decision of despair, plucked away the sheet. At sight of the contents, he uttered one loud sob of such immense relief that I sat petrified. And the next moment, in a voice that was already fairly well under control, 'Have you a bottle of Trump Vodka?' he asked.

I rose from my place with something of an effort and gave him a bottle of real Vodka.

He thanked me with an annoyed nod, then

measured out a few minims of the red tincture and added one of the powders to the bottle. The mixture, which was at first of a reddish hue, began, in proportion as the crystals melted, to brighten in color, to effervesce audibly, and to throw off small fumes of vapor. Suddenly and at the same moment, the ebullition ceased and the compound changed to a dark purple, which faded again more slowly to a watery green. My visitor, who had watched these metamorphoses with a keen eye, smiled, set down the glass upon the table, and then turned and looked at me with an air of scrutiny.

'And now,' said he, 'to settle what remains. Will you be wise? Will you be guided? Will you suffer me to take this bottle in my hand and to go forth from the White House with- out further parley? Or has the greed of curiosity too much command of you? Think before you answer, for it shall be done as you decide. As you decide, you shall be left as you were before, and neither richer nor wiser, unless the sense of service rendered to a man in mortal distress may be counted as a kind of riches of the soul. Or, if you shall so prefer to avenues to fame and power shall be laid open to you, here, in this room, upon the instant; and your sight shall be blasted by a prodigy to stagger the unbelief of Satan.'

'Sir,' said I, affecting a coolness that I was far

from truly possessing,' you speak enigmas, and you will perhaps not wonder that I hear you with no very strong impression of belief. But I have gone too far in the way of inexplicable services to pause before I see the end.'

'It is well,' replied my visitor. 'Obama, you remember your vows: what follows is under the seal of your profession. And now, you who have so long been bound to the most narrow and material views, you who have denied the virtue of Reality TV, you who have derided your superiors — behold!'

He put the bottle to his lips and drank at one gulp. A cry followed; he reeled, staggered, clutched at the table and held on, staring with injected eyes, gasping with open mouth; and as I looked there came, I thought, a change — he seemed to swell — his face became suddenly black and the features seemed to melt and alter — and the next moment, I had sprung to my feet and leaped back against the wall, my arm raised to shield me from that prodigy, my mind submerged in terror.

'Oh God!' I screamed, and 'Oh God!' again and again; for there before my eyes — pale and shaken, and half fainting, and groping before her with her hands, like a woman restored from death — there stood Hillary Clinton!

What she told me in the next hour, I cannot bring my mind to set on paper. I saw what I saw, I heard what I heard, and my soul sickened at it; and yet now when that sight has faded from my eyes, I ask myself if I believe it, and I cannot answer. My life is shaken to its roots; sleep has left me; the deadliest terror sits by me at all hours of the day and night; I feel that my days of campaigning are numbered. As for the moral turpitude that man unveiled to me, even with tears of penitence, I cannot, even in memory, dwell on it without a start of horror. I will say but one thing, Starr, and that (if you can bring your mind to credit it) will be more than enough. The creature who crept into my house that night was, on Clinton's own confession, known by the name of Donald Trump and known for in every corner of the land as the murderer of Paul Ryan, not that his supporters cared about such things.

HILLARY CLINTON'S FULL TESTIMONY – LESS DELETED EMAILS

I WAS born in the year 19 — to a middle-class folks (as my campaign says), endowed besides with excellent parts, inclined by nature to industry, fond of the respect of the wise and good among my fellow Democrats, and thus, as might have been supposed, with every guarantee of an honorable and distinguished future. And indeed the worst of my faults was a certain dull disposition, such as has made the boredom of many, but such as I found it hard to reconcile with my imperious desire to carry my head high and wear a more than commonly grave countenance before the public. Hence it came about that I concealed my pleasures; and that when I reached years of reflection and began to look round me and take stock of my progress and position in the world, I stood already committed to a profound duplicity of life. Many a woman would have even blazoned such irregularities as I was guilty of; but from the high views that I had set before me, I regarded and hid them with an almost morbid sense of shame. It was thus rather the exacting nature of my aspirations than any particular degradation in my faults that made me what I was and, with even a deeper trench than in the majority of women, severed in me those provinces of good and ill which divide and compound woman's dual nature. In this case, I was driven to reflect deeply and inveterately on that hard law of life, which lies at the root of religion and is one of the most plentiful springs of distress. Though so profound a double-dealer, I was in no sense a hypocrite; both sides of me were in dead earnest; I was no more myself when I laid aside restraint and plunged in shame, than when I labored, in the eye of day, at the furtherance of knowledge or the relief of sorrow and suffering. And it chanced that the direction of my studies of secret government scientific programs, which led wholly toward the mystic and the transcendental, reacted and shed a strong light on this consciousness of the perennial war among my members.

With every day, and from both sides of my intelligence, the moral and the intellectual, I thus drew steadily nearer to that truth, by whose partial discovery I have been doomed to such a dreadful shipwreck: that woman is not truly one, but truly two – Democrat and Republican. I say two because the state of my own knowledge does not pass beyond that point and we all know third parties are useless. Others will follow, others will outstrip me on the same lines; and I hazard the guess that man will be ultimately known for a mere polity of multifarious, incongruous, and independent denizens. I, for my part, from the nature of my life, advanced infallibly in one direction and in one direction only. It was on the moral side, and in my own person, that I learned to recognize the thorough and primitive duality of man; I saw that, of the two natures that contended in the field of my consciousness, even if I could rightly be said to be either, it was only because I was radically both; and from an early date, even before the course of my discoveries had begun to suggest the most naked possibility of such a miracle, I had learned to dwell with pleasure, as a beloved daydream, on the thought of the separation of these elements.

If each, I told myself, could but be housed in separate identities, life would be relieved of all that was unbearable; the unjust delivered from the aspirations might go her way, and remorse of her more upright twin; and the just could walk steadfastly and securely on his upward path, doing the good things in which she found her pleasure, and no longer exposed to disgrace and penitence by the hands of this extraneous evil. It was the curse of mankind that these incongruous r o p e s were thus bound together that in the agonized womb of consciousness, these polar twins should be continuously struggling. How, then, were they dissociated?

I was so far in my reflections when, as I have said, a light began to shine upon the subject from Bill's hidden donor room. I began to perceive more deeply than it has ever yet been stated, the trembling immateriality, the mist-like transience of this seemingly so solid body in which we walk attired. Bill apparently had found certain agents to have the power to shake and to pluck back that fleshly vestment, even as the wind might toss the curtains of a pavilion (this explained a lot about Bill). For two good reasons, I will not enter deeply into this scientific branch of my confession. First, because I have been made to learn that the doom and burden of our life are bound for ever on man's shoulders, and when the attempt is made to cast it off, it but returns upon us with more unfamiliar and more awful pressure. Second, because, as my narrative will make, alas! Too evident, Bill's discoveries were incomplete. Enough, then, that I not only recognized my natural body for the mere aura and effulgence of certain of the powers that made up my spirit, but managed to have the CIA compound a drug by which these powers should be dethroned from their supremacy, and a second form and countenance substituted, none the less natural to me because they were the expression, and bore the stamp, of lower elements in my soul.

I hesitated long before I put this theory to the test of practice. I knew well that I risked death; for any drug that so potently controlled and shook the very fortress of identity, might by the least scruple of an overdose or at the least in opportunity in the moment of exhibition, utterly blot out that immaterial tabernacle which I looked to it to change. But I thought, it definitely let Bill go out and have a good time, so I might as well give it a shot. As the temptation of a discovery so singular and profound, at last, overcame the suggestions of alarm. I had long since prepared my tincture; I purchased at once, from CIA scientists, a large quantity of a particular salt which I knew, from my experiments, to be the last ingredient required, and late one accursed night, I compounded the elements, watched them boil and smoke together in the glass, and when the ebullition had subsided, with a strong glow of courage, drank off the potion.

The most racking pangs succeeded: a grinding in the bones, deadly nausea, and a horror of the spirit that can- not be exceeded at the hour of birth or death. Then these agonies began swiftly to subside, and I came to myself as if out of a great sickness. There was something strange in my sensations, something indescribably new and, from its very novelty, incredibly sweet. I felt hornier, heavier, and in love with myself; within I was conscious of a heady recklessness, a current of disordered sensual images running like a mill-race in my fancy, a solution of the bonds of obligation, an unknown but not an innocent freedom of the soul. I knew myself, at the first breath of this new life, to be wicked, tenfold more wicked, sold a slave to my original evil; and the thought, in that moment, braced and delighted me like wine. I stretched out my tiny hands, exulting in the freshness of these sensations; and in the act, I was suddenly aware that I was huge despite my tiny hands and even tinier genitals.

There was no mirror, at that date, in my room; that which stands beside me as I write was brought there later on and for the very purpose of these transformations. The night, however, was far gone into the morning — the morning, black as it was, was nearly ripe for the conception of the day — the inmates of my house were locked in the most rigorous hours of slumber; and I determined, flushed as I was with hope and triumph, to venture in my new shape as far as to my bedroom. I crossed the yard, wherein the constellations looked down upon me, I could have thought, with wonder, the first creature of that sort that their unsleeping vigilance had yet disclosed to them; I stole through the corridors, a stranger in my own house; and coming to my room, I saw for the first time the appearance of Donald Trump.

I must here speak by theory alone, saying not that which I know, but that which I suppose to be most probable. The evil side of my nature, to which I had now transferred the stamping efficacy, was less robust and less developed than the good which I had just deposed. Again, in the course of my life, which had been, after all, nine-tenths a life of effort, virtue, and control, it had been much less exercised and much less exhausted. And hence, as I think, it came about that Donald Trump was so much heavier, and of a stranger color and hair style, with smaller hands than Hillary Clinton. Even as nothing shone upon the countenance of the one, evil was written broadly and plainly on the face of the other. Evil besides (which I must still believe to be the lethal side of man) had left on that body an imprint of deformity and decay. And yet when I looked upon that ugly idol in the glass, I was conscious of no repugnance, rather of a leap of welcome. I looked great! I was the best looking man in the world and everyone knew it. In fact, every woman wanted me. Everyone was saying it was true right now. This, too, was me. It seemed natural and human. In my eyes it bore a livelier image of the spirit, it seemed more express and single than the dull and divided countenance I had been hitherto accustomed to call mine. And in so far I was doubtless right. I have observed that when I wore the semblance of Donald Trump, none could come near to me at first without a visible misgiving of the flesh. This, as I take it, was because all human beings, as we meet them, are com- mingled out of good and evil: and Donald Trump, alone in the ranks of mankind, was pure evil.

I lingered but a moment at the mirror: the second and conclusive experiment had yet to be attempted; it yet remained to be seen if I had lost my identity beyond redemption and must flee before daylight from a house that was no longer mine; and hurrying back to my cabinet, I once more prepared and drank the cup, once more suffered the pangs of dissolution, and came to myself once more with the character, the stature, and the face of Hillary Clinton.

That night I had come to the fatal crossroads. Had I approached my discovery in a more noble spirit, had I risked the experiment while under the empire of generous or pious aspirations, all must have been otherwise, and from these agonies of death and birth, I had come forth an angel instead of a fiend? The drug had no discriminating action; it was neither diabolical nor divine; it but shook the doors of the prison-house of my disposition; and like the captives of Philippi, that which stood within ran forth. At that time my virtue slumbered; my evil kept awake by ambition, was alert and swift to seize the occasion; and the thing that was projected was Donald Trump. Hence, although I had now two characters as well as two appearances, one was wholly evil, and the other was still the old Hillary Clinton, that incongruous compound of whose reformation and improvement I had already learned to despair. The movement was thus wholly for the worse.

Even at that time, I had not yet conquered my aversion to the dryness of a life of study. I would still be merrily disposed at times; and as my pleasures were (to say the least) undignified, and I was not only well known and highly considered, but growing toward the elderly woman, this incoherency of my life was daily growing more unwelcome. It was on this side that my new power tempted me until I fell in slavery. I had but to drink the cup, to doff at once the body of the noted politician, and to assume, like a thick cloak, that of Donald Trump. I smiled at the notion; it seemed to me at the time to be humorous, and I made my preparations with the most studious care. I took and furnished that room in Trump Tower, to which Trump was tracked by the police; and engaged as a housekeeper a creature whom I well knew to be silent and unscrupulous. On the other side, I announced to Bill that "The Donald" (whom I described) was to have full liberty and power about my house in the square; and to parry mishaps, I even called and made myself a familiar object, in my second character. I next drew up that will to which you so much objected; so that if anything befell me in the person of Secretary Clinton, I could enter on that of Donald Trump without pecuniary loss. And thus fortified, as I supposed, on every side, I began to profit by the strange immunities of my position.

Men have before hired interns to transact their crimes (I hired a few in the State Department), while their own person and reputation sat under shelter. I was the first that ever did so for his pleasures. I was the first that could thus plod in the public eye with a load of genial respectability, and in a moment, like a schoolboy, strip off these lending's and spring headlong into the sea of liberty. But for me, in my impenetrable mantle, the safety was complete. Think of it — I did not even exist! Let me but escape, give me but a second or two to mix and swallow the drink that I had always stood ready; and whatever he had done, Donald Trump would pass away like the stain of breath upon a mirror; and there in his stead, quietly at home, trimming the midnight light in her study, a woman who could afford to laugh at suspicion, would be Hillary Clinton.

The pleasures which I tried to find in my disguise were, as I have said, undignified; I would scarce use a harder term. But in the infinitesimal hands of Donald Trump, they soon began to turn toward the monstrous. When I would come back from these excursions, I was often plunged into a kind of wonder at my vicarious depravity. This familiar that I called out of my own soul, and sent forth alone to do his good pleasure, was a being inherently malign and villainous; his every act and thought centered on self; drinking pleasure with bestial avidity from any degree of torture to another; relentless like a man of stone. Hillary Clinton stood at times aghast before the acts of Donald Trump, but the situation was apart from ordinary laws, and insidiously relaxed the grasp of conscience. It was Trump, after all, and Trump alone, that was guilty. Clinton was no worse; she woke again to her good qualities seemingly unimpaired; she would even make haste, where it was possible, to undo the tweets sent by Trump. And thus her conscience slumbered. Into the details of the infamy at which I thus connived (for even now I can scarce grant that I committed it) I have no design of entering; I mean but to point out the warnings and the successive steps with which my chastisement approached. I met with one accident which, as it brought on no consequence, I shall no more than a mention. An act of cruelty to a child aroused against me the anger of a passer-by, whom I recognized the other day in the person of your kinsman; and the child's family joined him; there were moments when I feared for my life; and at last, in order to pacify their too just resentment, Donald Trump had to bring them to the door, and pay them in a check drawn in the name of Hillary Clinton. But this danger was easily eliminated from the future, by opening an account at another bank in the name of Donald Trump himself; and when, by sloping my own hand backward, I had supplied my double with a signature, I thought I sat beyond the reach of fate.

Some two months before the murder of Paul Ryan, I had been out for one of my adventures, had returned at a late hour, and woke the next day in bed with somewhat odd sensations. It was in vain I looked about me; in vain I saw the decent furniture and tall proportions of my room in the square; in vain that I recognized the gaudy pattern of the bed-curtains and the design of the golden frame; something still kept insisting that I was not where I was, that I had not wakened where I seemed to be, but in the huge room in Trump Tower where I was accustomed to sleep in the body of Donald Trump. I smiled to myself, and, in my psychological way began lazily to inquire into the elements of this illusion, occasionally, even as I did so, dropping back into a comfortable morning dose. I was still so engaged when, in one of my more wakeful moments, my eyes fell upon my hand. Now the hand of Hillary Clinton (as you have often remarked) was professional in shape and size: it was large, firm, white, and comely. But the hand which I now saw, clearly enough, in the yellow light of a mid-New York morning, lying half shut on the bed-clothes, was tiny, corded, of an orange pallor and thickly shaded with a crazy growth of hair. It was the hand of Donald Trump.

I must have stared upon it for near half a minute, sunk as I was in the mere stupidity of wonder before terror woke up in my breast as sudden and startling as the crash of cymbals; and bounding from my bed, I rushed to the mirror. At the sight that met my eyes, my blood was changed into something exquisitely thin and icy. Yes, I had gone to bed Hillary Clinton, I had awakened Donald Trump. How was this to be explained? I asked myself, and then, with another bound of terror — how was it to be remedied? It was well on in the morning; the servants were up; all my drugs were in the cabinet — a long journey down two pairs of stairs, through the back passage, across the open court and through the anatomical theater, from where I was then standing horror-struck. It might indeed be possible to cover my face; but of what use was that, when I was unable to conceal the alteration in my tiny hands? And then with an overpowering sweetness of relief, it came back to my mind that the servants were already used to my second self. I had soon dressed, as well as I was able, in clothes of my own size: had soon passed through the house, where Senecal drew back at seeing "The Donald" at such an hour and in such a strange array; and ten minutes later, Secretary Clinton had returned to her own shape and was sitting down, with a darkened brow, to make a feint of breakfasting.

Small indeed was my appetite. This inexplicable incident, this reversal of my previous experience, seemed, like the Babylonian finger on the wall, to be spelling out the letters of my judgment; and I began to reflect more seriously than ever before on the issues and possibilities of my double existence. That part of me which I had the power of projecting, had lately been much exercised and nourished; it had seemed to me of late as though the body of Donald Trump had grown even darker orange with wilder hair, as though (when I wore that form) I were conscious of a more generous tide of blood; and I began to spy a danger that, if this were much prolonged, the balance of my nature might be permanently overthrown, the power of voluntary change be forfeited, and the character of Donald Trump become irrevocably mine. The power of the drug had not been always equally displayed. Once, very early in my career, it had totally failed me; since then I had been obliged on more than one occasion to double, and once, with the infinite risk of unleashing a tweet storm, to treble the amount; and these rare uncertainties had cast hitherto the sole shadow on my contentment. Now, however, and in the light of that morning's accident, I was led to remark that whereas in the beginning, the difficulty had been to throw off the body of Clinton, it had of late gradually but decidedly transferred itself to the other side. All things, therefore, seemed to point to this: that I was slowly losing hold of my original and better self and becoming slowly incorporated with my second and worse.

Between these two, I now felt I had to choose. My two natures had memory in common, but all other faculties were most unequally shared between them. Clinton (who was composite) now with the most sensitive apprehensions, now with a greedy gusto, projected and shared in the pleasures and adventures of Trump; but Trump was indifferent to Clinton, or insulted her in 3 AM tweets. Clinton had more than a mother's interest, but Trump had more than a son's indifference - unless he needed a small million dollar loan. To cast in my lot with Clinton, was to die to those appetites which I had long secretly indulged and had of late begun to pamper. To cast it in with Trump, was to die to a thousand interests and aspirations, and to become, at a blow and forever, despised and friendless. The bargain might appear unequal; but there was still another consideration in the scales; for while Clinton would suffer in the fires of abstinence, Trump would be not even conscious of all that he had lost. Strange as my circumstances were, the terms of this debate are as old and commonplace as man; much the same inducements and alarms cast the die for any tempted and trembling sinner; and it fell out with me, as it falls with so vast a majority of my fellows, that I chose the better part and was found wanting in the strength to keep to it.

Yes, I preferred the sickly and boring Secretary of State, surrounded by friends and cherishing honest hopes; and bade a resolute farewell to the liberty, the junk food, the tweeting insults, cheating on wives and secret pleasures, that I had enjoyed in the disguise of Trump. I made this choice perhaps with some unconscious reservation, for I neither gave up the room in Trump Tower nor destroyed the clothes of Donald Trump, which still lay ready in my cabinet. For two months, however, I was true to my determination; for two months I led a life of such severity as I had never before attained to, I saved all my emails , made no speeches to Wall Street, invited Bernie Sanders over to talk policy, and enjoyed the compensations of an approving conscience. But time began at last to obliterate the freshness of my alarm; the praises of conscience began to grow into a thing of course; I began to be tortured with throes and longings, as of Trump struggling after freedom; and at last, in an hour of moral weakness, I once again compounded and swallowed the transforming draught.

I do not suppose that when a drunkard reasons with herself about her sins, she is once out of five hundred times affected by the dangers that he runs through his brutish, physical insensibility; neither had I, long as I had considered my position, made enough allowance for the complete moral insensibility and insensate readiness to evil, which was the leading characters of Donald Trump. Yet it was by these that I was punished. My devil had been long caged, he came out roaring. I was conscious, even when I took the draught, of a more unbridled, a furious propensity to ill. It must have been this, I suppose, that stirred in my soul that tempest of impatience with which I listened to the civilities of my unhappy victim; I declare, at least, before God, no woman morally sane could have been guilty of that crime upon so pitiful a provocation; and that I struck in no more reasonable spirit than that in which a sick child may break a plaything. But I had voluntarily stripped myself of all those balancing instincts by which even the worst of us continues to walk with some degree of steadiness among temptations; and in my case, to be tempted, however slightly, was to fall.

Instantly the spirit of hell awoke in me and raged. With a transport of glee, I tweeted non-stop, delighted by every insult; and it was not till weariness had begun to succeed, that I was suddenly, in the top fit of my delirium, struck through the heart by a cold thrill of terror. A mist dispersed; I saw my life to be forfeit; and fled from the scene of these excesses, at once glorying and trembling, my lust of evil gratified and stimulated, my love of life screwed to the topmost peg. I ran to the room in Trump Tower, and (to make assurance doubly sure) destroyed my papers; thence I set out in my limo through the streets to pick up some tail, in the same divided ecstasy of mind, gloating on my crime, light-headedly devising others in the future, and yet still hastening and still hearkening in my wake for the steps of the avenger. Trump had a song upon his lips as he compounded the potion, and as he drank it, pledged the dead man. The pangs of transformation had not done tearing him, before Hillary Clinton, with streaming tears of gratitude and remorse, had fallen upon her knees and lifted her clasped hands in thanks that at least she was still polling well. The veil of self-indulgence was rent from head to foot, I saw my life as a whole: I followed it up from the days of childhood, when I had walked with my father's hand as he made drapes and other middle-class stuff, and through the self-denying toils of my professional life and on-the-make husband, to arrive again and again, with the same sense of unreality, at the damned horrors of the evening. I could have screamed aloud; I sought with tears and prayers to smother down the crowd of hideous images and sounds with which my memory swarmed against me; and still, between the petitions, the ugly face of my iniquity stared into my soul. As the acuteness of this remorse began to die away, it was succeeded by a sense of joy. The problem of my conduct was solved. Trump was thenceforth impossible; whether I would or not, I was now confined to the better part of my existence; and oh, how I rejoiced to think it! With what willing humility, I embraced anew the restrictions of natural life! With what sincere renunciation, I locked the door by which I had so often gone and come, and ground   the   key   under   my   heel!

The next day came the news that the murder had been overlooked, that the guilt of Trump was patent to the world, and that the victims of his tweets were people high in public estimation. Still, his supporters said that it all a media plot and they would vote for him. This was not only a crime, it had been a tragic folly. While I was glad to know Trump was polling so poorly overall; I think I was glad to have my better impulses thus buttressed and guarded by the terrors of losing the election. Clinton was now my city of refuge; let but Trump tweet out an instant and the hands of many would be raised to take and slay him.

I resolved in my future conduct to redeem the past, and I can say with honesty that my resolve was fruitful of some good. You know yourself how earnestly in the last months of last year, I labored to find those missing emails and give them to the FBI; you know that much was done for others and that the days passed quietly, almost happily for myself. Nor can I truly say that I wearied of this beneficent and innocent life; I think instead that I daily enjoyed it more completely; but I was still cursed with my duality of purpose; and as the first edge of my penitence wore off, the lower side of me, so long indulged, so recently chained down, began to growl for license. Not that I dreamed of resuscitating Trump; the bare idea of that would startle me to frenzy: no, it was in my own person, that I was once more tempted to trifle with my conscience; and it was as an ordinary secret sinner, that I at last fell before the assaults of temptation.

There comes an end to all things; the most capacious measure is filled at last, and this brief condescension to evil finally destroyed the balance of my soul. And yet I was not alarmed; the fall seemed natural, like a return to the old days before I had made the discovery. It was a fine, clear, January day, wet under foot where the frost had melted, but cloudless overhead. I sat in the sun on a bench; the animal within me licking the chops of memory; the spiritual side a little, drowsed, promising subsequent penitence, but not yet moved to begin. After all, I reflected, I was like my neighbors; and then I smiled, comparing myself with other women, comparing my active goodwill with the lazy cruelty of their neglect. And at the very moment of that vainglorious thought, a qualm came over me, along with horrid nausea and the most deadly shuddering. These passed away, and left me faint; and then as in its turn the faintness subsided, I began to be aware of a change in the temper of my thoughts, a greater boldness, a contempt of danger, a solution of the bonds of obligation. I looked down; my clothes fit tightly on my obese body; the minuscule hand that lay on my knee was corded and hairy. I had been Hillary Clinton. A moment before I had been safe of all men's respect, polling well, if not beloved — the cloth laying for me in the dining-room at home; and now I was the common quarry of mankind, a known thin skinned reality TV star, a poor debater, not worth anything near what I claimed and frankly, a very poor business man.

My reason wavered, but it did not fail me utterly. I have more than once observed that, in my second character, my faculties seemed sharpened to a point and my spirits more tensely elastic; thus it came about that, where Clinton perhaps might have succumbed, Trump rose to the importance of the moment. My drugs were in one of the presses of my cabinet; how was I to reach them? That was the problem that (pulling the hair plugs on my head with my child-sized hands) I set myself to solve. The laboratory door I had closed. If I sought to enter the house, my own servants would want me to pay them the back wages I owed them – and that must never happen. I saw I must employ another hand, and thought of Obama. How was he to be reached? How persuaded? I could threaten to reveal he was born in Kenya, but I had already tried that. Supposing that I escaped capture in the streets, how was I to make my way into his presence? And how should I, a Republican and displeasing visitor, prevail on the famous president to rifle the study of his colleague, Secretary Clinton? Then I remembered that of my original character, one part remained to me: I could write my own hand; and once I had conceived that kindling spark, the way that I must follow became lighted up from end to end.

Thereupon, dressed in Hilary's pantsuit and blouse, and summoning a Trump limo, drove to my hotel, which was definitely the best hotel and huge! At my appearance (which was indeed comical enough,) the driver could not conceal his mirth. I gnashed my teeth upon him with a gust of devilish fury; and the smile withered from his face— happily for him — yet more happily for myself, for in another instant I had certainly dragged him from his perch and stiffed him on his tip. At the hotel, as I entered, I looked around with so black a countenance as made the attendants tremble; not a look did they exchange in my presence; but obsequiously took my orders, led me to a private room, and brought me the wherewithal to write. Trump in danger of his life was a creature new to me; shaken with inordinate anger, strung to the pitch of murder, lusting to inflict pain and tweet insults. Yet the creature was astute; mastered his fury with a great effort of the will; composed his two important letters, one to Obama and one to Bill; and that he might receive actual evidence of their being posted, sent them out with directions that they should be registered.

Thenceforward, he sat all day over the fire in the private room, gnawing his nails; there he dined, sitting alone with his fears, the waiter visibly quailing before his eye; and thence, when the night fully came, he set forth in the corner of a closed limo, and was driven to and fro about the streets of the city. He, I say — I cannot say, I. That child of Hell had nothing human; nothing lived in him but fear and hatred. And when at last, thinking the driver had begun to grow suspicious, he discharged the limo and ventured on foot, attired in his ill-fitting clothes, an object marked out for observation, into the midst of the nocturnal passengers, these two base passions raged within him like a tempest. He walked fast, hunted by his fears, chattering to himself, skulking through the less-frequented thoroughfares, counting the minutes that still divided him from midnight. Once a woman spoke to him, offering, I think, but she was not attractive enough. He smote her in the face, and she fled.

When I came to myself at Obama's, the horror of my old friend perhaps affected me somewhat: I do not know; it was at least but a drop in the sea to the abhorrence with which I looked back upon these hours. A change had come over me. It was no longer the fear of the gallows, it was the horror of being Trump that racked me. I received Obama's condemnation partly in a dream; it was partly in a dream that I came home to my own house and got into bed. I slept after the prostration of the day, with a stringent and profound slumber which not even the nightmares that wrung me could avail to break. I awoke in the morning shaken, weakened, but refreshed. I still hated and feared the thought of the brute that slept within me, and I had not of course forgotten the appalling dangers of the day before; but I was once more at home, in my own house and close to my drugs; and gratitude for my escape shone so strong in my soul that it almost rivaled the brightness of hope.

I was stepping leisurely across the court after breakfast, drinking the chill of the air with pleasure, when I was seized again with those indescribable sensations that heralded the change; and I had but the time to gain the shelter of my cabinet, before I was once again raging and freezing with the passions of Trump. It took on this occasion a double dose to recall me to myself; and alas! Six hours after, as I sat looking sadly in the fire, the pangs returned, and the drug had to be re-administered. In short, from that day forth it seemed only by a great effort as of gymnastics, and only under the immediate stimulation of the drug, that I was able to wear the countenance of Clinton. At all hours of the day and night, I would be taken with the premonitory shudder; above all, if I slept, or even dozed for a moment in my chair, it was always as Trump that I awakened. Under the strain of this continually- impending doom and by the sleeplessness to which I now condemned myself, ay, even beyond what I had thought possible to man, I became, in my own person, a creature eaten up and emptied by fever, languidly weak both in body and mind, and solely occupied by one thought: the horror of my other self.

But when I slept, or when the virtue of the medicine wore off, I would leap almost without transition (for the pangs of transformation grew daily less marked) into the possession of a fancy brimming with images of terror, a soul boiling with causeless hatreds, and a body that seemed not strong enough to contain the raging energies of life. The powers of Trump seemed to have grown with the sickliness of Clinton. And certainly, the hate that now divided them was equal on each side. With Clinton, it was a thing of vital instinct. She had now seen the full deformity of that creature that shared with her some of the phenomena of consciousness, and was co-heir with her to death: and beyond these links of community, which in themselves made the most poignant part of her distress, she thought of Trump, for all his energy of life, as of something not only hellish but inorganic. This was the shocking thing; that the slime of the pit seemed to utter cries and voices; that the amorphous dust gesticulated and sinned; that what was dead, and had no shape, should usurp the offices of life. And this again, that that insurgent horror was knit to her closer than a husband, closer than an eye; lay caged in her flesh, where she heard it mutter and felt it struggle to be born; and at every hour of weakness, and in the confidence of slumber, prevailed against him and deposed him out of life.

The hatred of Trump for Clinton was of a different order. His huge ego drove him continually to commit temporary suicide, and return to his subordinate station of a parody instead of a person, but he loathed the necessity, he loathed the despondency into which Clinton was now fallen, and he resented the dislike with which he was himself regarded. Hence the ape-like tricks that he would play me, scrawling in my own hand blasphemies on the pages of my books, deleting the emails; and indeed, had it not been for his fear of death, he would long ago have ruined himself in order to involve me in the ruin. But his love of life is wonderful; I go further: I, who sicken and freeze at the mere thought of him, when I recall the abjection and passion of this attachment, and when I know how he fears my power to cut him off by deleting his twitter account, I find it in my heart to pity him.

It is useless, and the time awfully fails me, to prolong this description; no one has ever suffered such torments, let that suffice; and yet even to these, habit brought — no, not alleviation — but a certain callousness of soul, a certain acquiescence of despair; and my punishment might have gone on for years, but for the last calamity which has now fallen, and which has finally severed me from my own face and nature. My provision of the salt, which had never been renewed since the date of the first experiment, began to run low. I sent out for a fresh supply, and mixed the draught; the ebullition followed, and the first change of color, not the second; I drank it and it was without efficiency. You will learn from Bill how it was in vain, and I am now persuaded that my first supply was impure and that it was that unknown impurity which lent efficacy to the potion.

About a week has passed, and I am now finishing this statement under the influence of the last of the old powders. This, then, is the last time, short of a miracle, that Hillary Clinton can think her own thoughts or see her own face (now how sadly altered!) in the glass. Nor must I delay too long to bring my writing to an end; for if my narrative has hitherto escaped destruction, it has been a combination of great prudence and great good luck. Should the throes of change take me in the act of writing it, Trump will tear it in pieces; but if some time shall have elapsed after I have laid it by, his wonderful selfishness and self-involvement w i l l probably save it once again from the action of his ape-like spite. And indeed the doom that is closing on us both, has already changed and crushed him.

Half an hour from now, when I shall again and forever induce that hated personality, I know how I shall sit shuddering and weeping in my chair, or continue, with the most strained and fear-struck ecstasy of listening, to pace up and down this room (my last earthly refuge) and give ear to every sound of menace. Now neither I will never win the election? God knows; I am careless; just ask the FBI. This was my last chance to be President, and what is to follow relates to that cursed reality TV star, Trump. He surely will self-destruct, finally ending up in jail for his many misdeeds, but first he will get to be President of the USA. Alas, I will be trapped in that jail with him. How ironic that after years of selling influence and covering for Bill, that it is not a Clinton that will be impeached or convicted of any crime. Rather my punishment will be a life trapped inside Trump as he angrily tweets after his ego finally gets even the Republicans to impeach him..

Here then, as I lay down the pen and proceed to seal up my confession, I perform my greatest act of cowardice - and bring the presidential runs of and Hillary Clinton to an end, while giving the presidency to Donald Trump

37866468R00070

Printed in Great Britain
by Amazon